Robin Gill is Michael Ramsey Professor of Modern Theology at the University of Kent and an Honorary Provincial Canon of Canterbury Cathedral. He wrote the 2004 SPCK Lent Book, *A Sense of Grace*, and the 1992 Archbishop's Lent Book, *Gifts of Love*. At parish level he leads a clergy team serving five rural congregations in Kent and was formerly an Area Dean for seven years. Jenny, his wife, is a local GP and they have two children and four (wonderful) grandchildren.

A Bit Like Jesus

Robin Gill

First published in Great Britain in 2009

Society for Promoting Christian Knowledge
36 Causton Street
London SW1P 4ST

Copyright © Robin Gill 2009

All rights reserved. No part of this book may be reproduced or transmitted
in any form or by any means, electronic or mechanical, including
photocopying, recording, or by any information storage and retrieval
system, without permission in writing from the publisher.

SPCK does not necessarily endorse the individual views contained
in its publications.

Unless otherwise noted, Scripture quotations are taken from the
New Revised Standard Version of the Bible, Anglicized Edition,
copyright © 1989, 1995 by the Division of Christian Education
of the National Council of the Churches of Christ in the USA.
Used by permission. All rights reserved

British Library Cataloguing-in-Publication Data
A catalogue record for this book is available from the British Library

ISBN 978–0–281–06204–1

1 3 5 7 9 10 8 6 4 2

Typeset by Kenneth Burnley
Printed in Great Britain by Ashford Colour Press

Produced on paper from sustainable forests

Contents

Contents

Preface

The picture on the cover by the Indian artist Jyoti Sahi captures wonderfully well what this short Lent Book is struggling to achieve. I bought the original collage on a visit to his ashram near Bangalore. He depicts the Parable of the Sower. Yet it is an Indian Jesus who is the sower, wearing a Sikh turban and performing a Hindu dance as he scatters the seeds of faith. A practising Catholic, Jyoti Sahi is also splendidly ecumenical.

Once again this book is written for busy people. The same format as *A Sense of Grace* has been adopted. A short section is offered for every day, except Sunday, during the six weeks of Lent. The focus here is particularly on the healing stories and parables of Jesus (an academic account of them can be found in my 2006 book for Cambridge University Press, *Health Care and Christian Ethics*). However, there is also a new and more ecumenical feature. After each section there is a verse from the Jewish Psalms and the Muslim Qur'an (or Koran) for meditation. My hope is that faith can learn from faith at a time of some anxiety about religious fanaticism.

All biblical quotations come from the New Revised Standard Version and those from the Qur'an are based upon the Oxford World's Classics version interpreted by Professor Arthur J. Arberry (Oxford University Press).

This book has been road tested by the Anglican and Methodist churches in the Elham Valley, Kent. They very kindly asked me to give a series of lectures for Lent 2009 and then made really helpful comments and suggestions after each. Ruth McCurry from SPCK soon got wind of this and asked me to turn them into an SPCK Lent Book. My colleague Dr Alan Le Grys very generously read carefully through the whole script taking out some of the errors in my biblical analysis. And my wife Jenny patiently corrected some of my medical and pastoral observations.

I am immensely grateful to them all and must apologize for the many things that I am sure are still wrong. If they ever read the book, my students will love pointing them out!

I do hope that you enjoy reading *A Bit Like Jesus*. It has been a pleasure to write.

WEEK 1

Stories We Value

———⇒●⇐———

1

Understanding stories

Forty years ago our family spent a year in Papua New Guinea living in a remote area without roads. I was teaching in the theological college and Jenny was working in the local hospital. Our son was a toddler and our daughter just a baby. We lived in a tin-roofed shack with occasional electricity from a generator. Toads, geckoes, spiders and hundreds of mosquitoes lived under the same roof.

And we came back to the West with stories galore about our exotic gap year . . . stories that we have recounted ever since.

I also collected traditional stories. The British anthropologist Charles Gabriel Seligman had visited the area in 1904, just three decades after Anglican missionaries first arrived. He recorded several of the stories that the local people still told. Stories about coconuts becoming human heads (they do look a bit like heads), about rats and butterflies that made canoes, about giant pigs that ate people, about boys spearing fish and then turning into fish themselves. Stories that must have been handed down from generation to generation.

The theological students that I taught all spoke Wedau, the local language. Despite, or perhaps because of, the myriad of languages in Papua New Guinea, new students soon learned it. So, as part of a teaching project on cultural change, I asked them to interview the local villagers, young and old, recording the stories still circulating almost seven decades after Seligman's visit.

Did the villagers still tell the same stories as their ancestors?

Yes and no. The older villagers knew all of the stories in one form or another. There was one man, probably in his late eighties, who may even have been in the village when Seligman visited. He had a remarkable memory for stories. The young, in contrast, knew only some – usually the ruder ones.

Memory of the more complicated stories was undoubtedly beginning to fade. Even in the remembered stories small details had changed subtly over time. A canoe that in Seligman's time set out to sea now simply crossed a river, and a kite became a small bird. Odd details changed in puzzling ways.

It was particularly fascinating that the 'meaning' of many stories told to the students had changed radically from the meaning (or, more usually, lack of meaning) recorded by Seligman. Little morals or explanations had been attached to stories that previously lacked them. For example, a rat that was buried in the early version was now eaten by a crow, with an explanation that that was how birds originally became flesh-eaters. Another story had turned into an explanation about how people first became cannibals (a practice thankfully long extinct in this area).

Looking at these changes helps us to understand how oral stories work. Unlike written stories that, precisely because they are written down, might remain constant over long periods of time, oral stories can change quite quickly. Of course, there may even have been several versions of the same story in Seligman's time. Perhaps he relied too heavily on single informants. Or perhaps contact with Westerners had unintentionally changed the details and meaning of traditional stories.

It might be a feature of enduring stories that they carry many different meanings and can be read by people from a wide range of perspectives. Stories that can appeal to different ages and to different age groups might be more likely to survive than stories that cannot.

If this is so, then perhaps one of the most important questions to ask about a story is simply 'Who is the listener?' or 'Who is the reader?'

———⟫●⟪———

MEDITATION

Psalm 104.4

You make the winds your messengers,
fire and flame your ministers.

Sura 7.175

So relate the story; haply they will reflect.

2

Healing stories and parables

Can I make an assumption about you as a reader of this Lent Book? I may well be wrong, but I assume that you are slightly intrigued by what it means to be 'a bit like Jesus'. I should explain.

Emphatically I do not think that even the most dedicated follower of Jesus really is 'just like Jesus'. For years I was reluctant to call myself 'a Christian', even though from the age of five I wanted to be ordained and took a very active part in the local church. For me such a claim felt much too presumptuous. Instead I used to say, 'I am trying to be a Christian.' Nor was I very enamoured of those who proclaimed loudly that they were Christians or, even worse, that they were saved. Surely God alone knows such things.

Yet times change. Those claiming to be atheists are now more strident, and churchgoers have become a minority. So I sometimes lapse into the language of talking about myself as 'a Christian'. Not without some twinges of regret. I would still prefer God alone to decide whether or not I really am a Christian.

If you share such misgivings the phrase 'a bit like Jesus' may mean something to you. It assumes that our messy lives are in many respects not much like Jesus. At most we can aspire just sometimes to be a bit like Jesus, or, more accurately, to be weak channels of some of the values that Jesus showed in such abundance.

I am also writing this Lent Book for those of you who would not even go that far. You may be puzzled by faith and trying to discover for yourself what values Jesus really did hold and demonstrate in his life.

You might even belong to a faith that already values Jesus, but not as God. For Muslims Jesus is a Prophet. For Jews he is a Son of Israel. For many Humanists Jesus is an important ethical teacher. I hope that I write for you as well. Together we can learn. That is why the Meditation at the end of each section uses a verse from both the Jewish Psalms and the Muslim Qur'an.

There is already a hint here of what is to come. I will be looking at stories, particularly in the first three Gospels (Mark, the earliest, and Matthew and Luke who both knew Mark's Gospel). Some of these stories are about Jesus and some are stories that Jesus told – a mixture of stories, mostly healing stories, and parables. And my aim is to unpick from these stories the values that are present within them. Some of these values are explicit within the stories, but some are more hidden. They all have much to teach us.

One of the great discoveries of biblical scholars in the early twentieth century was that for the first three Gospel writers the 'kingdom of God' or the 'kingdom of Heaven' (the two phrases meant the same in Hebrew) was central to the message of Jesus. In other parts of the New Testament the kingdom of God is seldom mentioned, but in these three Gospels it occurs over one hundred times. A preface to several of Jesus' parables in these Gospels is as follows: 'The kingdom of God is like . . .' And healing stories are sometimes presented as signs that the kingdom of God is already present in the work of Jesus. In contrast, there is little about the Church in these Gospels.

There is widespread agreement that the kingdom of God is not usually to be seen in spatial terms. In English 'kingdom' often denotes a place (although just occasionally it is used in a non-spatial sense, as in the phrase 'the animal kingdom'). In the Gospels it typically denotes the kingship, reign, rule or (perhaps better today) the active presence of God. This active presence is demonstrated in these Gospels in the life and teaching of Jesus. It was present but it was also depicted as future. Both now and yet to come. The Gospel writers believed that something extremely important was already happening and would go on happening in and through Jesus.

Some have argued that all the parables in these Gospels were originally about the kingdom of God, whether this is given explicitly in the text as their meaning or not. There is much dispute about this.

It would be impertinent of me even to attempt to resolve this dispute here. Obviously the kingdom of God is important, although my particular focus will be upon the values of this kingdom. Kingdom values, if you will, or perhaps just gospel values. That is sufficient for the moment.

However, there is another crucial point to make at this stage. Important questions can be raised about the origin of stories, but that is not their only feature. There are also questions about their ongoing meaning. Just as the oral stories in Papua New Guinea accrued new meanings in a later generation, so the parables of Jesus may have already started to accrue fresh meanings when they were first committed to papyrus by the Gospel writers. What is more, they continue to accrue new meanings as they are retold today.

That is the fascinating feature of stories. Perhaps that is why Jesus taught through stories. His stories continue to intrigue us today. We continue to puzzle over them and to find new and unexpected meanings within them.

Stories are important.

———⟶⟶●⟵⟵———

MEDITATION

Psalm 78.1–3

Give ear, O my people, to my teaching;
incline your ears to the words of my mouth.
I will open my mouth in a parable;
I will utter dark sayings from of old,
things that we have heard and known,
that our ancestors have told us.

Sura 6.25

When they come to you they dispute with you, the unbelievers saying, 'This is naught but the fairy-tales of the ancient ones.'

3

Family stories

Stories are particularly important for families. We tell and retell stories about where and when we were born, about holidays shared, about birthday and Christmas parties enjoyed long ago, about grandparents and great-grandparents no longer with us, about pets and houses that we once owned. Stories are deeply important for shaping families. Stories help bind us together.

An aunt who lived to the age of 99 had an astonishing memory. Unlike the rest of us she could remember even the smallest details of family events both recent and long past. As she grew older she loved to recall these events again and again. Even though we had heard her do this time after time we quickly forgot the finer details. So each time we had to ask her. Just who was this particular cousin? What was the grandmother's maiden name? And where exactly did they live? Right to the end she could remember.

Then she was gone. She never did want to be 100. After 65 years of marriage she wanted to be with 'my old dear, wherever he is now'.

It is when elderly relatives die that we can discover just how important family stories are. When they are alive the telling and retelling of the same stories easily becomes routine, even irksome. Something that the elderly frequently do and the young should patiently accept. However, when they die we think of all the things that we should have asked them, or the things that we did ask them and have now forgotten. A part of the family has gone with them.

Perhaps that is why so many of us get interested in family history as we grow older. Go into any local history library and you will find dozens of people in their 60s and 70s searching through micro-films of old baptism, marriage and burial records. The more adventurous will then write family histories and perhaps even record their own childhood memories for their grandchildren or yet-to-be-born great-grandchildren. For our fortieth wedding anniversary that is exactly what we did. Perhaps in 60 years' time our grandchildren will read our record and do the same for their children and grandchildren.

Even the discovery of long-hidden family secrets is greeted with interest. 'So that is why they got married', or 'So he died in a hostel for alcoholics.' It is all part of the family story. It is a part of what we are ourselves. It is *our* story.

Since my father came from Gibraltar his family history is wonderfully circumscribed. Until fairly recently, though, the local archives were not open to the general public. Now they are. After many pleasurable (and occasionally frustrating) hours of research I have been able to discover things about the Gibraltar Gills that my father and grandfather would have loved to have known. They only had access to records held in the Catholic Cathedral in Gibraltar and from these they assumed that the Gills were Catholics, originally coming as shopkeepers from Ireland in the early nineteenth century. In reality William Gill was a wheelwright who came as a young man from Kent to Gibraltar at the time of Trafalgar, and was not a Catholic at all. His wife Jane was born and baptized as an Anglican in Gibraltar in 1785; her parents had come there during the Great Siege with the army from the Scottish Borders. All absolutely fascinating to me and to my family but of little interest to you as a reader.

Family stories are just that. They are *family* stories, of little or no relevance to anyone else but of great interest within the family itself. Such stories are intimately connected with family identity. Even just knowing the names of long-dead relatives helps to give a sense of identity.

My grandfather never knew his own father. He died three months before my grandfather, himself an only child, was born. He had a portrait of his father and grandfather (both shopkeepers in Gibraltar) and a few photographs of his father, but he knew little about them. His devoted mother spoke only Spanish and knew little about the English side of the family. But she did pass on their love and pride to my grandfather. In turn he became a much-loved family doctor in Gibraltar and a devoted parent and grandparent. Even the few family stories that he did receive through his mother were important in shaping his life.

Stories help to bind families together and to pass on values from one generation to another.

As do the stories told about Jesus and the stories that Jesus told.

Yet there is a problem.

———⟫●⟪———

MEDITATION

Psalm 128.3

Your wife will be like a fruitful vine
within your house;
your children will be like olive shoots
around your table.

Sura 4.40

Be kind to parents.

4

Healing stories rather than miracle stories

The problem is that many will see the Gospel stories as miracle stories. So are they really healing stories?

Here, for example, is the first such story in Mark 1.21–28:

> They went to Capernaum; and when the sabbath came, he entered the synagogue and taught. They were astounded at his teaching, for he taught them as one having authority, and not as the scribes. Just then there was in their synagogue a man with an unclean spirit, and he cried out, 'What have you to do with us, Jesus of Nazareth? Have you come to destroy us? I know who you are, the Holy One of God.' But Jesus rebuked him, saying, 'Be silent, and come out of him!' And the unclean spirit, throwing him into convulsions and crying with a loud voice, came out of him. They were all amazed, and they kept on asking one another, 'What is this? A new teaching – with authority! He commands even the unclean spirits, and they obey him.' At once his fame began to spread throughout the surrounding region of Galilee.

Immediately after this story Jesus went to Simon's house and healed his mother-in-law who had a fever, and then in the evening 'he cured many who were sick with various diseases, and cast out many demons; and he would not permit the demons to speak, because they knew him' (v. 34).

Traditionally these are all seen as 'miracles' and not simply as 'healings'.

Much depends here upon the reader. Some will indeed interpret these as miracles, although the Greek word 'miracle' is not used here. The story does say that the people were 'amazed',

10

but then they were also 'astounded' at Jesus' teaching. Again, those who interpret these as miracles may not agree with each other about what constitutes a miracle. Many different definitions of 'miracles' have been offered. A miracle might simply be seen as 'a wonder', or as 'an event that does not conform to the normal run of human experience', or (with Aquinas) as 'what is done by divine power, which, being infinite, is incomprehensible in itself'.

Yet all of these definitions cause problems. In earlier times events might appear as a wonder, as not conforming to human experience, or as incomprehensible. In contrast, today they may seem more mundane.

There is a very real danger that we read these stories through twenty-first-century eyes. For us miracles (if we think that they happen) are usually seen as very rare and exotic. Thousands of people go to Lourdes every year but the doctors there very seldom claim that miraculous cures have happened. And for us today there is nothing particularly unusual about a fever lifting or about schizophrenics going into remission. Even the distinction between 'healing' and 'curing' that we typically make today is not made in any of the Gospel stories. To take Lourdes again, many pilgrims who go there find this to be a healing experience even though they are not actually cured from their illness or disability. In modern medicine the term 'cure' demands a much higher standard of explanation and proof than would have been possible or expected in the ancient world.

These are complex points, and readers will decide differently about them. However, whether you see the stories as miracles or not, my suggestion is that we can also see them as healing stories that tell us about values in everyday life. They can tell us about the values that Jesus in the Gospels held and that, in turn, we should hold ourselves, however feebly.

Read in this way, the question of what actually happened in the Gospel stories using modern medical terms becomes less important. In any case, it is seldom possible to answer this question adequately because we are simply not given the clinical details that any doctor today would expect before making a diagnosis. We are handling stories from the first century, not looking at a textbook of scientific medicine. We should not treat the stories as manuals for a working doctor in the twenty-first century. Instead, more significantly, we can treat them as stories that tell us all about what it is to be a bit like Jesus.

Such a way of looking at these stories fits the story above surprisingly well. The story, after all, makes a direct link between Jesus' teaching in the synagogue 'with authority' and his healing the man with an unclean spirit 'with authority'. The teaching and the healing are at one in the story. The healing becomes part of the teaching.

In short, the values of the kingdom are present in the whole life story of Jesus . . . in both his teaching and healing.

MEDITATION

Psalm 19.1

The heavens are telling the glory of God;
and the firmament proclaims his handiwork.

Sura 10.5

In the alternation of night and day, and what God has created in the heavens and the earth – surely there are signs for a God-fearing people.

5

Life stories

On my shelves I have an inherited collection of original Henty novels. Written for boys in Victorian England they remained popular in the early twentieth century and are still collectable today. G. A. Henty was a self-taught historian who wrote heroic novels based loosely upon famous events in the past in order to edify young people. As a child I remember reading them with great excitement. As an adult, sadly, they now appear appallingly racist and imperialist.

We have changed. Once biographies were largely uncritical and deferential. They told us about the lives of the great and the good and they invited us to admire and emulate them. Even politicians were treated with respect and politeness when interviewed on radio or early television.

Not so today. Politicians are typically grilled by interviewers as if they are all self-serving, lying cheats. We have become suspicious and cynical about those in positions of authority and power, whether in politics, in business, in churches or even in the media itself. Ironically, broadcasters and journalists may have increased our cynicism both about others and about themselves.

Modern biographies about 'heroes' of the past often seek to debunk them and reveal their feet of clay. We learn all about their sexual behaviour or their financial intrigues. About how they were terrible parents or unfaithful husbands or wives. About their neglect of the poor or about their rampant egotism.

That is if we are even concerned to read about people from the past. Go into almost any bookshop today and the shelves marked 'biographies' are likely to be written by, for or about recent 'celebrities' instead. Celebrity culture, even celebrity veneration, now appears to dominate.

Yet there is still one small area where more edifying life stories can be found. Obituaries. I am an avid reader of thoughtful obituaries. Not so much the often guilt-ridden obituary notices in local newspapers. They can indeed be interesting, especially if they need to be decoded (cynicism again). 'Fun-loving', for example, can be a polite euphemism for alcoholic, or 'plain-speaking' for intolerably rude.

Instead it is the obituaries in the more thoughtful national newspapers that I most enjoy. Once dead a whole life can be seen. That person can add no more. Obituaries at their best offer glimpses of whole life stories.

As I write, *The Times* carries an obituary of Patrick Kinna who has just died aged 95. Evidently he was a very modest man who had remarkable gifts as a confidential assistant and short-hand writer to Winston Churchill during the war. He had a shorthand speed of 150 words per minute and could take down dictation straight on to a typewriter at 50 words per minute. His talents were spotted and he was recommended to Churchill at a vexed stage in the war. Adoring Churchill, he was tactful and discreet. He could also cope with Churchill's nocturnal lifestyle. Sleeping in a room next to Churchill he was frequently woken in the middle of the night to record his latest thoughts.

In retirement Patrick Kinna gave talks about his wartime experiences and characteristically donated the money received to charity. The obituary captures something of both his life and that of Churchill in his more private moments.

Just to give a single example:

Kinna was a witness to many incidents that have passed into history. On the visit to Washington at Christmas 1941 he was summoned to Churchill's bathroom in the White House. 'I went in with my notebook and there was Mr Churchill in the bath, bobbing up and down like a porpoise, saying a few words and then going down again. When he got out of the bath, his valet dried him as best he could but Mr Churchill wouldn't stay still, so the valet wrapped him in the towel.

'The Prime Minister was still dictating as he walked up and down in his adjoining bedroom and in no time the towel had fallen off and he was starkers. Suddenly, there was a knock on the door and Mr Churchill said: "Come in". And who should it be but the President of the United States in his wheelchair.

'Mr Churchill always found the right thing to say, and on this occasion it was: "You see, Mr President, I have nothing to hide from you."' (*The Times*, 19 March 2009)

The modest and dutiful assistant and the charismatic but less than modest Prime Minister.

We can still learn from the stories of others' lives even if we have become more worldly wise about their shortcomings. Perhaps biographies and interviews in the past were too deferential even if in the present they tend to be too cynical. Thoughtful obituaries, no longer concerned to expose the frailties of the living, can offer something in between these extremes.

And we can indeed learn from the various Gospel stories about Jesus – stories, as we shall see, full of interesting tensions. Sometimes they are quite disturbing and at other times encouraging. Yet all were written to foster faith, not cynicism.

They are life stories to be valued.

———⟫●⟪———

MEDITATION

Psalm 105.26–27

He sent his servant Moses,
and Aaron whom he had chosen.
They performed his signs among them.

Sura 2.80

And We gave to Moses the Book, and after him sent succeeding Messengers; and We gave Jesus son of Mary the clear signs, and confirmed him with the Holy Spirit.

6

Values from stories

Why did Jesus not give us a set of moral laws? I suspect that for many of us it would have been so much easier had he done so.

Imagine for a moment that the Gospels were full of moral laws, dos and don'ts, like parts of Leviticus in the Old Testament. So, every time we had a debate about some important ethical issue, all that we had to do was look up the appropriate moral law. Instead of having endless debates within churches about issues such as homosexuality, euthanasia, market economics or climate change, all that we had to do would be to look up the moral law that Jesus taught.

To be even more helpful (especially to academics) Jesus might also have produced a systematic moral theory upon which the moral laws were founded. Following such ancient Greek philosophers as Aristotle and Plato, Jesus might have left a definitive moral theory for his followers to abide by. Problem solved.

Well, perhaps not entirely. It would have been difficult for Jesus in the first century to have left clear and understandable moral laws about, say, GM crops or testing the DNA of newborn babies. Many ethical issues in the twenty-first century arise from discoveries that were unknown in the first century. Much of health-care ethics today falls into this category.

However, these issues aside, Jesus might at least have left definitive moral laws about the perennial dilemmas facing every generation of human beings. Perhaps an expanded version of the Ten Commandments. That would have been helpful.

Instead of which Jesus left elusive stories, especially in the first three Gospels. Even the Fourth Gospel, which contains far fewer stories, does not actually contain clear-cut moral teaching. Rather, it has elaborate and extended metaphors about vines, sheepfolds and so forth. Every bit as elusive.

Of course, even if Jesus had left all of this we would still have problems. Laws need to be interpreted. Is, for example, withdrawing life-sustaining treatment from someone euthanasia or not? Is a committed and faithful same-sex relationship really to be equated with promiscuous homosexuality (let alone with pederasty)? Within religious traditions that inherit detailed moral laws there is soon found to be a need for authoritative interpretations of those laws.

Even when asked to set out a moral law Jesus in Luke's Gospel refrained from doing so. We shall be returning to the Parable of the Good Samaritan later. For the moment this is how the parable is introduced:

> Just then a lawyer stood up to test Jesus. 'Teacher,' he said, 'what must I do to inherit eternal life?' He said to him, 'What is written in the law? What do you read there?' He answered, 'You shall love the Lord your God with all your heart, and with all your soul, and with all your strength, and with all your mind; and your neighbour as yourself.' And he said to him, 'You have given the right answer; do this, and you will live.'
>
> But wanting to justify himself, he asked Jesus, 'And who is my neighbour?' Jesus replied, 'A man was going down from Jerusalem to Jericho . . .' (Luke 10.25–30)

The lawyer (like all subsequent readers) is forced to work out through the parable that follows just what is involved in loving your neighbour as yourself. Doubtless it would have been so much more clear-cut and comforting had Jesus articulated a detailed moral law at this stage.

Yet it is the parable that has lived with us and that has inspired novels, great paintings and altruistic deeds. It is the parable that has been told and retold and that has even become embedded in the name of the Samaritans today, the charity seeking to bring counselling to those who are desperate and suicidal. The phrase 'acting the good Samaritan' also remains as a term of approval within a society that may have largely forgotten its original context or the tensions between first-century Israelites and Samaritans.

The stories of Jesus continue to shape lives, and not just of those who are explicitly seeking to be a bit like Jesus. They have even wider resonance.

I have a standing joke with an atheist colleague who is a professor of Moral Philosophy. He is inclined to say that I do not have any rational grounds for my belief in God. My response is to tease him back by claiming that he does not have any rational grounds as a Humanist for his moral values, he just borrows them off me. Neither of us of course would accept these accusations. Yet there is sufficient truth in them to ensure that we do not spend our entire time wrangling about God. Instead we have happily worked together around the university encouraging other colleagues to take research ethics seriously whatever their religious or philosophical beliefs.

I doubt if I can convince him about God until and unless he feels some need for God in his life. You can lead people to a place of prayer but you cannot force them to pray. Yet I am still delighted that we can share together values that resonate with those contained in the stories of Jesus.

The chapters that follow are going to identify five values that are particularly important in these stories. The first is a sharp negative value, hypocrisy. The subsequent values are all positive: compassion, care, faithfulness and humility. Taken together they make strong demands upon those of us striving to be a bit like Jesus.

———⟫●⟪———

MEDITATION

Psalm 49.3–4

My mouth shall speak wisdom;
the meditation of my heart shall be understanding.
I will incline my ear to a proverb;
I will solve my riddle to the music of the harp.

Sura 10.20

The Unseen belongs only to God. Then watch and wait: I shall be with you watching and waiting.

WEEK 2

Hypocrisy

⟨━━⟩➤●◄⟨━━⟩

7

Jesus and the disabled woman

Now he was teaching in one of the synagogues on the sabbath. And just then there appeared a woman with a spirit that had crippled her for eighteen years. She was bent over and was quite unable to stand up straight. When Jesus saw her, he called her over and said, 'Woman, you are set free from your ailment.' When he laid his hands on her, immediately she stood up straight and began praising God. But the leader of the synagogue, indignant because Jesus had cured on the sabbath, kept saying to the crowd, 'There are six days on which work ought to be done; come on those days and be cured, and not on the sabbath day.' But the Lord answered him and said, 'You hypocrites! Does not each of you on the sabbath untie his ox or his donkey from the manger, and lead it away to give it water? And ought not this woman, a daughter of Abraham whom Satan bound for eighteen long years, be set free from this bondage on the sabbath day?' When he said this, all his opponents were put to shame; and the entire crowd was rejoicing at all the wonderful things that he was doing. (Luke 13.10–17)

Taken at face value this story, told only by Luke, seems to be incredibly unfair. Given the importance of the Sabbath for Jews the synagogue leader's repeated indignation appears to be so obviously right. The woman had had her disability (whatever its cause) for 18 years. One more day in the interests of keeping the Holy Sabbath surely would not have mattered. Jesus might reasonably have upheld the Sabbath and come back the following day to heal her.

Of course it is possible (as some scholars believe) that Jesus was determined to challenge the Jewish Law in any way possible. In the very first chapter of Mark Jesus healed twice on the Sabbath. On the other hand, as will be seen later, in this same chapter of Mark Jesus also told the healed leper to keep 'what Moses commanded' (v. 44). There is a tension here to be explored in another chapter.

There is a good deal of anger and passion in a number of the healing stories. However, this story in Luke contains a particularly sharp rebuke. The leader of the synagogue and the crowd were denounced by Jesus:

'You hypocrites!'

Firmly put in their place, they were then reminded about the small concessions for domestic animals on the Sabbath that were allowed by at least some Jewish authorities (although in reality some were harsher at the time). Surely these religious people could have done at least as much for a fellow human being?

Yet the charge of 'hypocrisy' still seems harsh. These were, after all, religious people who were attempting to fulfil their sacred duty. Perhaps they could have made a concession on the Sabbath, but Jesus himself could just as easily have made a concession about healing and waited one more day. There was some point to the logic that 'there are six days on which work ought to be done; come on those days and be cured, and not on the sabbath day'.

This objection may miss some of the deliberate irony in this story, set as it is by Luke in the midst of a set of parables about the kingdom. The story can perhaps best be seen as a kind of acted parable. It does indeed read like a stage drama:

- The woman is strongly depicted as 'crippled for eighteen years'
- She 'was bent over and was quite unable to stand up straight'
- Once healed she 'stood up straight and began praising God'
- Those in the synagogue were starkly denounced as 'hypocrites'
- Jesus depicted her graphically as 'a daughter of Abraham whom Satan bound for eighteen long years'
- And he pleaded that she should 'be set free from this bondage on the sabbath day'
- At the end 'his opponents were put to shame'
- And the *entire* crowd was 'rejoicing at all the wonderful things that he was doing'.

By telling the story in this dramatic way Luke was able to emphasize the charge of 'hypocrisy'. The previous chapter had already given some stark warnings about this:

Meanwhile, when the crowd gathered in thousands, so that they trampled on one another, he began to speak first to his disciples, 'Beware of the yeast of the Pharisees, that is, their hypocrisy. Nothing is covered up that will not be uncovered, and nothing secret that will not become known. Therefore whatever you have said in the dark will be heard in the light, and what you have whispered behind closed doors will be proclaimed from the housetops.' (Luke 12.1–3)

The language here about 'covering' and 'uncovering' is apt, as is the dramatic language of the healing story. In classical Greek the word 'hypocrite' was used, without any criticism intended, for an actor. Acting in Greek plays involved wearing masks, enabling the covered-up actor to pretend to be, and to be seen by the audience to be, the character in the play. It is not too difficult to see how this sense of the word eventually took on a more negative tone as it still does in the English language today.

The hypocrite now becomes the one who pretends *in real life* to be something positive but actually is quite the opposite. No longer acting in the make-believe world of the theatre, but acting (while pretending not to be acting) in the real world.

It is quite difficult to find a single meaning that fits exactly every use of the term 'hypocrite' in the Gospels. Often it involves a deliberate pretence or 'covering', but not always. In Luke's story of the synagogue leader and crowd their hypocrisy may not have been deliberate at all. Their hypocrisy here seems to be that they saw themselves as religiously observant and pious while ignoring the 'bondage' of the 'daughter of Abraham'.

Precisely because this story is directed at the religiously observant it becomes so fearfully relevant to those of us who are churchgoers or temple-goers today. It directs at us the charge of 'hypocrisy' – a charge that the world at large is also all too ready to direct at today's religiously active.

We have been warned.

We religious people do have a sad tendency towards hypocrisy.

———

MEDITATION

Psalm 135.16–17

They have mouths, but they do not speak;
they have eyes, but they do not see;
they have ears, but they do not hear,
and there is no breath in their mouths.

Sura 4.140

The hypocrites seek to trick God.

8

Religious hypocrisy

This accusation against religious people is especially strong in the first three Gospels. Within the New Testament the term 'hypocrite' is found only in these Gospels. It is always found on the lips of Jesus himself. And it is typically directed at the religiously active and their leaders.

The word 'hypocrite' is used four times in Luke and no fewer than 13 times in Matthew. Most famously, Matthew places it firmly in the Sermon on the Mount:

'Beware of practising your piety before others in order to be seen by them; for then you have no reward from your Father in heaven.

'So whenever you give alms, do not sound a trumpet before you, as the hypocrites do in the synagogues and in the streets, so that they may be praised by others. Truly I tell you, they have received their reward. But when you give alms, do not let your left hand know what your right hand is doing, so that your alms may be done in secret; and your Father who sees in secret will reward you.

'And whenever you pray, do not be like the hypocrites; for they love to stand and pray in the synagogues and at the street corners, so that they may be seen by others. Truly I tell you, they have received their reward. But whenever you pray, go into your room and shut the door and pray to your Father who is in secret; and your Father who sees in secret will reward you . . .

'And whenever you fast, do not look dismal, like the hypocrites, for they disfigure their faces so as to show others that they are fasting. Truly I tell you, they have received their reward. But when you fast, put oil on your head and wash your face, so that your fasting may be seen not by others but by your Father who is in secret; and your Father who sees in secret will reward you.' (Matthew 6.1–6, 16–18)

Note the threefold structure typical of traditional stories. Three ways that the religiously active can become hypocrites, that is, 'practising your piety before others in order to be seen by them': through ostentatious alms-giving, through prayer 'in the synagogues and at the street corners', and through public fasting.

All of these practices performed hypocritically as a display to fellow human beings rather than as a private devotion to God. Even more insidiously, all of them misused as a means of gaining human praise rather than as a personal act of thanksgiving to God. Ostentatious humility, if you will, the abiding temptation of many a religious leader. If you are truly humble you may (thankfully with some important exceptions) never be noticed and thus never picked to be a leader. Yet if you are not seen to be humble you may never be chosen either. So, somehow, potential religious leaders need to be spotted by others for their humility . . . hence ostentatious humility.

Hardly surprising that Jesus, at least as he is portrayed in Matthew and Luke, is so critical of religious leaders.

This passage from the Sermon on the Mount (with a missing section as indicated by the dots above) is set as an option for Ash Wednesday in *The Common Worship Lectionary*. If it is indeed read and if the service also includes a mark of ashes on the forehead, it has sometimes caused me problems. Do I go out into the world with an ostentatious mark on my forehead? Or do I quickly wipe it off as I leave the church?

Perhaps in un-churched Britain today it makes little difference. Few may be aware of the significance of the ashes or even that it is Ash Wednesday. And the few who do notice may themselves have been similarly marked. However, in the rich religious pluralism of Gibraltar – with very observant Catholic, Muslim and Sephardic Jewish communities – my Ash Wednesday dilemma was more acute. I swiftly wiped the ashes off. The Gospel reading was just too insistent. Or perhaps I was being over-sensitive.

Just what is the missing section in this reading? I asked this question in a Lent group when preparing this book. There was a silence. Then someone remembered: 'It's the Lord's Prayer.' It is indeed:

'When you are praying, do not heap up empty phrases as the Gentiles do; for they think that they will be heard because of their many words. Do not be like them, for your Father knows what you need before you ask him.

'Pray then in this way:

Our Father in heaven,
hallowed be your name . . .' (Matthew 6.7–9)

The central prayer of Christian worship, sandwiched by Matthew (but not Luke) in between admonitions against religious hypocrisy.

An important reminder about proper religious practice – albeit framed by practices that are not a bit like Jesus.

—————➤●◄—————

MEDITATION

Psalm 69.10–11

When I humbled my soul with fasting,
they insulted me for doing so.
When I made sackcloth my clothing, I became a byword to them.

Sura 63.1

When you see [hypocrites], their bodies please you: but when they speak, you listen to their speech, and it is as they were propped-up timbers.

9

Hypocrisy and paedophile priests

Forget about my petty scruples concerning Ash Wednesday. It is time to take a much stronger example of religious hypocrisy. For instance, the shameful way that for generations senior clergy in a number of churches covered up for their actively paedophile colleagues.

It is important not to exaggerate. Some have claimed that active paedophilia has long been rife within churches. I am aware of no evidence to suggest that this is the case, although of course by definition checkable evidence in this area is unlikely. It is sufficient to point out that there are now a number of well-documented cases involving priests who have been convicted in the courts of paedophile abuses and are currently serving prison sentences. There is also clear evidence about senior clergy at one stage or another covering up the criminal actions of these clergy. That is sufficient.

How could this possibly have happened? The answer is only too obvious. Church leaders saw their primary duty as being to protect the reputation of their church rather than to help the victims of paedophilia. Perhaps they also believed (or wanted to believe) the claims of the clergy who had abused young people, namely that they would never do so again. Yet here too they placed their duty to fellow clergy ahead of their duty to the young victims.

They may also have thought that by moving the clergy involved to another environment or to work that involved less contact with young people they were acting compassionately. Here again their compassion was directed to their abusive colleagues rather than to the original victims or even to potential victims in the new environment. In other words, they were prepared to risk other young people in order to protect both their colleagues and the reputation of their church.

There is nothing particularly unusual about institutions protecting their own. Church leaders are not alone in doing this. Harold Shipman raised the suspicion of a number of his doctor colleagues while he was murdering dozens of vulnerable patients. They noticed the abnormally high death rates in his practice and the unusual way that several patients actually died in his surgery. Some even relayed their misgivings to others. But surely caring doctors don't do such things? And his patients loved him. So nothing was done until he crudely forged the will of an elderly victim whose daughter happened to be a lawyer.

Compared with cases like these the synagogue leader and crowd charged with hypocrisy by Jesus in Luke seem to be almost innocent. Yet common to them all is a lack of compassion to those most in need. Public scruples were given priority over compassion for the vulnerable.

Church leaders may not be alone in covering up for predatory colleagues, but many might hope that their moral standards would be higher. That does seem to be the force of Jesus' condemnation of religious leaders in Matthew: 'for the sake of your tradition, you make void the word of God. You hypocrites!' (15.6–7).

This surely is why tabloid newspapers take such relish in exposing the hypocritical behaviour of religious leaders. Scurrilous though these newspapers might sometimes be, they do nevertheless have a vital role here. Leaders in all areas, especially those in positions of power and responsibility, do need to be held to account when their actions harm vulnerable people.

Slowly church leaders have learned to change their ways. After a number of public scandals, court cases and successful claims for major damages in several countries, it is now more properly realized that the victims of paedophilia should always be given priority. Suspected perpetrators should be referred at once to the police rather than moved sideways within churches.

Once again a dramatic parable makes this point about priority so effectively:

When the Son of Man comes in his glory, and all the angels with him, then he will sit on the throne of his glory. All the nations will be gathered before him, and he will separate people one from another as a shepherd separates the sheep from the goats, and he will put the sheep at his right hand and the goats at the left. Then the king will say to those at his right hand, 'Come, you that are blessed by my Father, inherit the kingdom prepared for you from the foundation of the world; for I was hungry and you gave me food, I was thirsty and you gave me something to drink, I was a stranger and you welcomed me, I was naked and you gave me clothing, I was sick and you took care of me, I was in prison and you visited me.' Then the righteous will answer him, 'Lord, when was it that we saw you hungry and gave you food, or thirsty and gave you something to drink? And when was it that we saw you a stranger and welcomed you, or naked and gave you clothing? And when was it that we saw you sick or in prison and visited you?' And the king will answer them, 'Truly I tell you, just as you did it to one of the least of these who are members of my family, you did it to me.' Then he will say to those at his left hand, 'You that are accursed, depart from me into the eternal fire prepared for the devil and his angels; for I was hungry and you gave me no food, I was thirsty and you gave me nothing to drink, I was a stranger and you did not welcome me, naked and you did not give me clothing, sick and in prison and you did not visit me.' Then they also will answer, 'Lord, when was it that we saw you hungry or thirsty or a stranger or naked or sick or in prison, and did not take care of you?' Then he will answer them, 'Truly I tell you, just as you did not do it to one of the least of these, you did not do it to me.' And these will go away into eternal punishment, but the righteous into eternal life. (Matthew 25.31–46)

The stark final verse of this parable serves to emphasize the importance of striving to be a bit like Jesus.

Failing to give priority to the vulnerable is not a bit like Jesus.

———➤●◄———

MEDITATION

Psalm 103.15–17

As for mortals, their days are like grass;
they flourish like a flower of the field;
for the wind passes over it, and it is gone,
and its place knows it no more.
But the steadfast love of the LORD is from everlasting to everlasting
on those who fear him,
and his righteousness to children's children . . .

Sura 76.1

We created man of a sperm-drop, a mingling, trying him; and
We made him hearing, seeing. Surely We guided him upon the
way whether he be thankful or unthankful.

10

Hypocrisy and AIDS

Within the Parable of the Sheep and the Goats both those who did and those who did not give priority to the vulnerable are mystified. 'Lord, when was it that we saw you hungry and gave you food, or thirsty and gave you something to drink? And when was it that we saw you a stranger and welcomed you, or naked and gave you clothing? And when was it that we saw you sick or in prison and visited you?'

Just as the synagogue leader and crowd appeared astounded at the charge of hypocrisy, so the unrighteous in this parable were amazed to be condemned for their lack of action for the vulnerable. Not all those charged with hypocrisy in the Gospels were aware that they were hypocrites. Insidiously many religious hypocrites, then and now, may actually be convinced that they act righteously while simultaneously 'covering up' or ignoring evidence to the contrary.

This may well explain the charge of hypocrisy levelled at some religious and secular leaders when first confronted by the AIDS pandemic. The charge was made at several levels.

Initially in the West AIDS was thought to be solely a gay disease. Not surprisingly some of the most reactionary religious leaders soon proclaimed it to be God's punishment upon the gay community. Some of them quoted Leviticus to support this:

You shall not lie with a male as with a woman; it is an abomination. (18.22)

If a man lies with a male as with a woman, both of them have committed an abomination; they shall be put to death; their blood is upon them. (20.13)

So presumably God was directly putting gay people to death through the AIDS pandemic. Unfortunately, of course, it was soon realized that straight people could also contract the disease. A divine punishment intended for one group had sadly affected another. Yet it was still thought to be gay people who were responsible for this. It was claimed that it was through sinful gay behaviour that the wives and then the children of bisexual men acquired AIDS.

Gradually it began to be realized that AIDS world-wide is not solely or even primarily a gay disease. With millions of people now being HIV positive in Sub-Saharan Africa AIDS was reconfigured by these religious leaders as a punishment from God for sexual promiscuity, straight or gay. Again its victims extended well beyond the sexually promiscuous themselves: haemophiliacs, health-care workers with needle stick injuries, newborn babies, continent wives of promiscuous husbands, and many others. Yet it was still seen by some as a divine punishment.

At this stage various political and religious leaders started also to contest the claims of scientists working in this area. Some claimed that there was no relationship between HIV and AIDS. Some believed the claims made by traditional healers to have a cure for the disease. Others argued that their country was exempt from the pandemic. Or they argued that condoms were no barrier to acquiring the disease. Denial, covering up and hypocrisy were rife in many different forms.

As I write, another form of hypocrisy is only now beginning to crumble in Africa with the realization that some clergy are HIV positive. A few courageous Anglican priests have now come out, admitting that they too are HIV positive and encouraging others to do the same. Slowly churches are beginning to be aware that some of those living with HIV are also leading their worship.

Over the last few years I have become increasingly engaged in this area. UNAIDS, the Joint United Nations Programme concerned with reducing HIV infection and treating people living with AIDS, came to realize that theologians and church leaders might be able to change attitudes, shape values, encourage truth-telling within churches and break down appalling messages about AIDS as a divine punishment. It will be seen in section 22 that the healing stories of Jesus have been particularly important in trying to achieve all of this.

There must surely be ways of thinking about AIDS that are a bit more like Jesus.

———➤●◄———

MEDITATION

Psalm 146.3–4

Do not put your trust in princes,
in mortals, in whom there is no help.
When their breath departs, they return to the earth;
on that very day their plans perish.

Sura 2.5

They would trick God and the believers, and only themselves they deceive, and they are not aware.

11

Practise what you preach

Those who regularly deliver sermons in church should live in fear of this proverb. It might have been designed for us. Do we really live up to what we preach?

A common factor in many of the uses of the word 'hypocrite' in the first three Gospels involves a severe gap between preaching and practice, or between our stated beliefs and practices and what we actually do in our lives – whether we are aware of these yawning gaps or not. This is made explicit in the advice to the crowds in Matthew about the scribes and Pharisees: 'Do whatever they teach you and follow it; but do not do as they do, for they do not practise what they teach' (23.2–3).

The earliest Gospel writer captures this gap in his single reference to hypocrisy:

> So the Pharisees and the scribes asked him, 'Why do your disciples not live according to the tradition of the elders, but eat with defiled hands?' He said to them, 'Isaiah prophesied rightly about you hypocrites, as it is written,
>
> > "This people honours me with their lips,
> > but their hearts are far from me;
> > in vain do they worship me,
> > teaching human precepts as doctrines."
>
> You abandon the commandment of God and hold to human tradition.' (Mark 7.5–8)

It is also present in a familiar parable told by both Matthew and Luke. Here is Luke's version:

He also told them a parable: 'Can a blind person guide a blind person? Will not both fall into a pit? A disciple is not above the teacher, but everyone who is fully qualified will be like the teacher. Why do you see the speck in your neighbour's eye, but do not notice the log in your own eye? Or how can you say to your neighbour, "Friend, let me take out the speck in your eye", when you yourself do not see the log in your own eye? You hypocrite, first take the log out of your own eye, and then you will see clearly to take the speck out of your neighbour's eye.' (Luke 6.39–42)

Once again there is a strong use of irony and deliberate exaggeration in this parable. The speck in the neighbour's eye is contrasted with the whole log (as if!) in your own eye. The hypocrite has not even noticed this log or the grotesque way that it distorts his vision. That is how ridiculous such hypocrisy is.

And then there is the deliberate form of hypocrisy captured in Matthew's wonderfully obsequious story leading up to Jesus using a coin to demonstrate what should be given to the emperor or instead to God:

Then the Pharisees went and plotted to entrap him in what he said. So they sent their disciples to him, along with the Herodians, saying, 'Teacher, we know that you are sincere, and teach the way of God in accordance with truth, and show deference to no one; for you do not regard people with partiality. Tell us, then, what you think. Is it lawful to pay taxes to the emperor, or not?' But Jesus, aware of their malice, said, 'Why are you putting me to the test, you hypocrites? . . . (Matthew 22.15–18)

Whenever lecturing I am always wary of those in the audience who use all of my academic titles before reaching their question. The latter is almost certain to be tricky or abusive or both. Note the carefully structured mock deference in Matthew ahead of the actual question:

- Teacher
- we know that you are sincere
- and teach the way of God in accordance with truth
- and show deference to no one
- you do not regard people with partiality

Tell us, then . . .

The questioners pretended to be sincere truth-seekers, whereas in reality they were deliberately setting a trap. If Jesus in the story had suggested giving all to the emperor, he could have been seen as a collaborator (as presumably were the Herodians themselves) or even as an idolater (the emperor was after all worshipped by Romans). If, rather, he had insisted upon everything going to God, he might instead have been identified by the Romans as a tax evader. Caught both ways.

Deliberate hypocrisy.

—————

MEDITATION

Psalm 12.2

They utter lies to each other;
with flattering lips and a double heart they speak.

Sura 6.65

Those who take their religion for a sport and a diversion.

12

Learning from hypocrisy

Gene Robinson, the elected Bishop of New Hampshire, was not invited to attend the 2008 Lambeth Conference of Bishops. It was considered that his committed but gay partnership would make his presence too offensive to others within the Anglican Communion.

As an outright opponent of what he believes to be Anglican hypocrisy Gene Robinson was never likely to be deterred from coming to Canterbury and being visibly present while the other Lambeth Bishops deliberated there. So he came in considerable style and received more media attention than he might had he been invited in the first place.

Since the Lambeth Conference met on the university campus where I work I could not resist going to one of the lectures that he gave there on the very fringe of the conference itself. It was sponsored by the university's law school and attracted a large audience of academics and church leaders.

He is a very skilled speaker. Relaxed, friendly, funny and persuasive. Many of us were much impressed by his performance. He spoke at length about the debates that he has had both within his own Church, the Episcopal Church of the United States of America, and within the wider Anglican Communion. And he was highly critical of both, arguing that Christians are far too prone to discrimination against gays and other minority groups. Clearly he regarded it as deeply hypocritical that he, an open gay, had not been invited to the conference whereas others who were closet gays had been. In addition, he argued, he was a democratically elected bishop whereas again others at the conference were not. The Church had much to answer for.

Questions were generally polite until one academic stood and declared: 'I'm an atheist. You evidently consider Christians to be just as dreadful as I do, so why don't you join me?'

At this point Gene Robinson became less than coherent, losing much of his relaxed, friendly, funny and persuasive delivery. He also started talking in religious clichés.

Clearly he had not expected this point to be made. I suspect that he imagined that he was talking to a familiar church audience, well used to being told about our various shortcomings. Instead he was speaking in a secular British university and to a mixed secular and religious audience. A relentlessly negative critique of the churches had been heard by the secular minded simply as a confirmation of their own position.

If this Lent Book stopped at this point it would have fallen into a similar trap. It would be yet another book showing that religious people are a rotten lot and not at all like Jesus. However, that would have missed this book's intention entirely. Hypocrisy has been an important initial theme precisely because it is so prevalent on Jesus' lips in the first three Gospels. It is in the earliest Gospel, Mark, in the common stories shared by Matthew and Luke, and in the unique stories told separately by Matthew and Luke. So it does need to be taken very seriously. It does have a very strong claim to represent a central element in Jesus' own teaching.

Yet this negative critique is just a preparation. It clears the stage or cleanses the system (apologies for a mixed metaphor). It allows us first to recognize a human tendency, shared doubtlessly by the religious and non-religious alike, and then to seek to move beyond it – albeit realizing that it is likely to return just when we are at our most self-satisfied.

Hypocrisy has this much in common with pride. Hypocrisy, like pride, often starts with laudable principles. Pride has the advantage that we can properly talk, for example, about people having pride in their work. Yet both seduce us into ostentation, into pretending in public that we are better than we are. It is worth remembering that the Victorian novelist Anthony

Trollope deliberately named one of his most pompous clerics Mr Proudy.

So, if we are wise, we seek hard to avoid this seduction and to avoid public pretension. Then, just when we begin to make progress in this direction, we feel some pride that we have done so . . .

The sad cycle of hypocrisy and pride.

Whether or not mortals ever can truly move beyond this cycle, the Gospel stories of and about Jesus point us to more positive values as well: compassion, care, faith and humility. It is these positive values that will form the focus of the rest of this Lent Book.

Together they offer a positive, albeit demanding, vision of what it is to be a bit like Jesus.

MEDITATION

Psalm 84.10

For a day in your courts is better
than a thousand elsewhere.
I would rather be a doorkeeper in the house of my God
than live in the tents of wickedness.

Sura 76.25

Remember the name of your LORD at dawn and in the evening and part of the night; bow down before him and magnify him through the long night.

WEEK 3

Compassion

⟶⟶●◁⟶

13

Healing and compassion

As they were leaving Jericho, a large crowd followed him. There were two blind men sitting by the roadside. When they heard that Jesus was passing by, they shouted, 'Lord, have mercy on us, Son of David!' The crowd sternly ordered them to be quiet; but they shouted even more loudly, 'Have mercy on us, Lord, Son of David!' Jesus stood still and called them, saying, 'What do you want me to do for you?' They said to him, 'Lord, let our eyes be opened.' Moved with compassion, Jesus touched their eyes. Immediately they regained their sight and followed him. (Matthew 20.29–34)

Many of the healing stories in the first three Gospels begin as this story does. A vulnerable person (here two people) sees Jesus nearby and calls out for 'mercy' or 'pity' and Jesus responds. In this particular story from Matthew the two blind men are extremely persistent, so much so that the crowd becomes angry. The men, in turn, shout again, emphasizing their plea for 'mercy' even more forcefully.

Neither the word 'mercy' nor 'pity' quite captures the sense of the Greek word used here. 'Mercy' in English usually has judicial connotations, as it does sometimes in Greek. The prisoner, once found guilty, pleads for 'mercy' from the judge before sentence is pronounced. Guilt has already been established so a plea for mercy is a plea for lenient punishment. This is seldom appropriate for healing stories in the Gospels. Guilt or sin are seldom mentioned in these stories.

'Pity' also presents problems in English. It often has rather patronizing connotations. When we pity someone we typically do so from a position of privilege. We pity the poor or people with serious disabilities because we, thankfully, are not poor or have no such disabilities. Those who are poor or disabled, on the other hand, may not be quite so grateful for our pity. They might well prefer our respect.

For these reasons some biblical scholars argue that it is more appropriate to use the English word 'compassion' to translate the Greek word used by the blind men in Matthew's story. So their plea to Jesus becomes instead: 'Have compassion on us, Lord, Son of David!'

That does fit Jesus' response in this story. He was 'moved with compassion'. This time the more usual Greek verb for compassion is used. In Greek it has a highly visceral meaning, referring to the guts or entrails. Something rather stronger than 'gut feeling', more like 'his guts or entrails heaved'. In the ancient world the guts were often thought to be the location of our deepest emotions.

The Latin from which the word 'compassion' itself is derived captures some of this meaning. It can be translated as 'suffering alongside' someone or even feeling 'with passion'. This is not just empathy, trying to put yourself into someone else's shoes. It involves action as well as just feeling. If I claim to be compassionate about those in need but do nothing for them, others are likely to consider that I am not really compassionate at all.

Compassion properly understood involves three inter-linked responses: identifying someone as being in real need, feeling strongly for that person, and then being determined to help that person in any way possible.

Understood in this way compassion and justice are two sides of the same coin. If compassion tends to focus upon needy people nearby, justice has a wider concern for the needy across the world.

The story can now take on a new energy:

- Two blind men heard that Jesus was passing by
- They shouted, 'Lord, have compassion on us, Son of David!'
- The crowd (lacking compassion) sternly ordered them to be quiet
- But they shouted even more loudly, 'Have compassion on us, Lord, Son of David!'
- Jesus stood still and called them, saying, 'What do you want me to *do* for you?'
- They said to him, 'Lord, let our eyes be opened.'
- Moved with compassion, Jesus touched their eyes
- Immediately they regained their sight and followed him.

———————

MEDITATION

Psalm 145.9

The LORD is good to all,
and his compassion is over all that he has made.

Sura 1.1

In the name of God, the Merciful, the Compassionate.
Praise belongs to God, the LORD of all Being, the All-merciful,
the All-compassionate.

14

The Parable of the Prodigal, his Brother and their Compassionate Father

Then Jesus said, 'There was a man who had two sons. The younger of them said to his father, "Father, give me the share of the property that will belong to me." So he divided his property between them. A few days later the younger son gathered all he had and travelled to a distant country, and there he squandered his property in dissolute living. When he had spent everything, a severe famine took place throughout that country, and he began to be in need. So he went and hired himself out to one of the citizens of that country, who sent him to his fields to feed the pigs. He would gladly have filled himself with the pods that the pigs were eating; and no one gave him anything. But when he came to himself he said, "How many of my father's hired hands have bread enough and to spare, but here I am dying of hunger! I will get up and go to my father, and I will say to him, 'Father, I have sinned against heaven and before you; I am no longer worthy to be called your son; treat me like one of your hired hands.'" So he set off and went to his father. But while he was still far off, his father saw him and was filled with compassion; he ran and put his arms around him and kissed him. Then the son said to him, "Father, I have sinned against heaven and before you; I am no longer worthy to be called your son." But the father said to his slaves, "Quickly, bring out a robe – the best one – and put it on him; put a ring on his finger and sandals on his feet. And get the fatted calf and kill it, and let us eat and celebrate; for this son of mine was dead and is alive again; he was lost and is found!" And they began to celebrate.

'Now his elder son was in the field; and when he came and approached the house, he heard music and dancing. He called one of the slaves and asked what was going on. He replied, "Your brother has come, and your father has killed the fatted calf, because he has got him back safe and sound." Then he became angry and refused to go in. His father came out and began to plead with him. But he answered his father, "Listen! For all these years I have been working like a slave for you, and I have never disobeyed your command; yet you have never given me even a young goat so that I might celebrate with my friends. But when this son of yours came back, who has devoured your property with prostitutes, you killed the fatted calf for him!" Then the father said to him, "Son, you are always with me, and all that is mine is yours. But we had to celebrate and rejoice, because this brother of yours was dead and has come to life; he was lost and has been found."' (Luke 15.11–32)

This is the longest and most elaborate parable or story and it is found only in Luke. The Gospel writer adds no 'explanation' of it, despite explanations being given of the two shorter parables placed immediately before it. Perhaps along with other good stories it really does not need any explanation. As it stands it has inspired many great works of art and literature and, like them, been given many different interpretations.

For some this is a story about forgiveness and repentance. For others it is a story about a loving father. Or it is seen as a story about unexpected redemption and new life. Or a story about two brothers, one wayward and the other jealous. The rich literary details of this skilfully told story add to its complexity and tantalizing elusiveness. Luke is the great story teller.

For me it is the central verse that is particularly interesting: 'But while he was still far off, his father saw him and was filled with compassion; he ran and put his arms around him and kissed him.' It is again the strong, visceral Greek word that is translated here as 'filled with compassion'. Not just that, but the father 'ran and put his arms around him [literally, 'fell on his neck'] and kissed him'.

The three inter-linked responses of compassion can be seen in the father's response. He saw the once wayward and truculent son (the one who had brusquely demanded 'give me the share of the property that will belong to me') as now being in real need. He responded with strong, physically expressed emotion. And he acted immediately: 'Quickly, bring out a robe – the best one – and put it on him; put a ring on his finger and sandals on his feet. And get the fatted calf and kill it, and let us eat and celebrate; for this son of mine was dead and is alive again; he was lost and is found!'

In sharp contrast the elder brother is not the least bit compassionate. His response has shaped the English language and is beautifully captured in this translation, especially those phrases that I have put into italics: 'Listen! For all these years *I have been working like a slave for you*, and I have never disobeyed your command; yet you have never given me even a young goat so that I might celebrate with my friends. *But when this son of yours* came back, who has devoured your property with prostitutes, *you killed the fatted calf for him*!'

The compassionate father and the less than compassionate son.

———⟫●⟪———

MEDITATION

Psalm 112.4–5

They rise in the darkness as a light for the upright;
they are gracious, merciful, and righteous.
It is well with those who deal generously and lend,
who conduct their affairs with justice.

Sura 4.40

Be kind . . . to orphans and to the needy, and to the neighbour who is of kin, and to the neighbour who is a stranger, and to the companion at your side, and to the traveller.

15

Compassion in health care

Some of the new and exciting developments in medical science – especially in the area of genetics and stem cell research – raise complex ethical issues. Developments in patient care also raise old problems in new forms. For instance, modern medicine seems to be capable of keeping people alive well beyond the point that many of us would wish. There are also major problems about priorities and even rationing. Should health services devote as many costly and scarce resources to the elderly as they do to the young?

Today medical ethics is an essential part of the training of doctors and nurses and there are numerous medical ethics committees to address the challenges that they face in their work and research. I am very privileged to be a member of several of these, albeit usually as the only theologian present. Of course some of the doctors, nurses and scientists on these committees may be privately religious, yet this cannot be assumed. There are also lawyers and philosophers present, some of whom are explicitly hostile to religion in any form. So what is the role of a theologian in this context?

Perhaps a theologian is there to oppose secular forms of ethics. Many decisions are made by such committees quite pragmatically by attempting to balance the risks involved in a particular form of treatment (all surgery and most medication do involve risks) with their benefit to the patient. There is also considerable discussion about patient autonomy, examining whether or not patients have been properly informed about the proposed treatment, given a free choice about having or not having it, and assured about confidentiality. All of this is now standard fare in medical ethics. Should a theologian be opposing it?

My answer is firmly 'no'. I do not believe that theologians have a monopoly of wisdom in ethics and I do want all health-care workers to act ethically, whether they are personally religious or not. I also believe that it would be irresponsible not to attempt to balance the risks and benefits of treatment, and unethical not to share this information properly with patients themselves.

So I do strongly support such considerations on medical ethics committees. What then is a theologian doing specifically on these committees? Does she or he have anything distinctive to add to their deliberations?

Perhaps a theologian is there to represent religious minorities. Conservative Jews, Catholics and Muslims are all likely to have pro-life views at odds with current medical practices relating to the beginning and end of life. For example, traditional Catholics are unlikely to agree with IVF in any form, or with barrier and hormonal means of contraception. Or possibly it is the demands of more sectarian groups that the theologian should be trying to represent. For example, the strong objection to blood transfusions by Jehovah's Witnesses. A religiously pluralist society does need to be aware of groups that object conscientiously to otherwise widely accepted medical practices.

Yet my experience is that in reality most medical ethics committees are well aware of such conscientious objections and argue that (for adult patients at least) they must be respected. They are aware that doctors giving a blood transfusion to a Jehovah's Witness patient would from her perspective endanger her prospects of eternal life. For many adult Jehovah's Witnesses it is much better to die prematurely in this world than to lose the possibility of life in the next. That is precisely why Jehovah's Witnesses were so courageous and unbreakable in Hitler's concentration camps or in Stalin's gulags. Threats in this world were as nothing compared with the prospect of rewards in the next.

A rather better explanation of the role of a theologian on medical ethics committees today may involve values. I share the values about autonomy, risks and benefits, and am pleased that many committees also consider issues concerned with wider justice. Yet I believe that there are some values involved in good medical practice that are not always well represented in ethical discussion. Compassion is one of these. Subsequent chapters will suggest that care, faith and humility are others. It will be proposed that these gospel values do still have an important contribution to make even in wider society today.

Compassion *is* sometimes mentioned in medical ethics. Yet it is seldom the explicit starting point and frequently it is swamped by other values. Some of my more robust secular colleagues even regard 'compassion' as being just too soft and irrational to be of much use in medical ethics. A few even dismiss compassion as a 'slave value'. In contrast, I believe that it should have priority.

Whenever doctors and nurses are asked about why they chose to train for their profession in the first place they frequently mention compassion. Cynics might claim that money was their prime motivation. Or, less cynically, that popular acclaim was crucial: 'This is my daughter, she is a doctor', or 'That is my son, he is a nurse'. However, doctors and nurses themselves often mention compassion, perhaps as a result of an early experience of compassionate healing or of a wider conviction about wanting to help those who are vulnerable.

It is widely considered that doctors or nurses who lack compassion are not good doctors or nurses. Many still talk about them as belonging to 'caring professions'. Like the clergy they are regularly given high ratings by the general public as people who care and can be trusted. And when a Dr Shipman is discovered people are deeply shocked.

Of course doctors and nurses should be trained properly, and need to be knowledgeable about medical science. People today do want them to respect their autonomy as patients and to give them proper choices about the risks and benefits of treatment. Yet they also want them to be compassionate and caring human beings. They want them to be concerned about their patients as people and not just as objects of medical curiosity.

Compassion is not an optional extra for health-care workers.

Compassion is crucial and central.

————➤●◄————

MEDITATION

Psalm 63.3

Because your steadfast love is better than life,
my lips will praise you.

Sura 10.55

In the bounty of God, and his mercy – in that let them rejoice.

16

Compassion and assisted suicide

If compassion really is crucial and central should we not legalize assisted suicide in Britain? As I write, this question is being frequently asked in newspapers, magazines and on television. For some years Dignity in Dying (in the past it was called The Voluntary Euthanasia Society) has campaigned in the media on behalf of those wishing to change the current law. Very properly this organization has brought a succession of tragic cases to public attention and argued consistently that a change in law is required on compassionate grounds.

I believe that they have a strong case, but I am not finally persuaded that it is safe actually to change the law.

However, Professor Paul Badham, a friend and fellow theologian, is convinced about changing the law. In his very recent and readable book he presents the compassionate case well:

> The importance of outgoing unselfish, loving compassion for others is often claimed as one of the greatest contributions that Christianity has given to the world . . . It is celebrated in St Paul's great hymn to love in 1 Corinthians 13, one of the best loved of all biblical passages. It is highly relevant to the euthanasia debate . . . when a person is suffering unbearably during their terminal illness and repeatedly begs for assistance to die. It is hard to see how anyone who takes St Paul's praise of loving compassion seriously could fail to respond to the desperate cries for help witnessed by Dr Julia Lawton in her account of individual patients' experiences of palliative care. Among the more tragic were Christine, suffering from unrelievable chronic diarrhoea, which made her describe life in the hospice as 'the nearest thing to hell on earth', or Kath who

begged for permanent sedation because 'no one would put a dog through this' or Roz who experienced the hospice as a 'death factory'. When people's sufferings are so great that they make repeated requests to die, it seems a denial of that loving compassion, which is supposed to be the hallmark of Christianity, to refuse to allow their requests to be granted. (Paul Badham, *Is There a Christian Case for Assisted Dying?*, SPCK, London, 2009, pp. 120–1)

Paul Badham might also have referred to the story from Luke 13 about 'Jesus and the disabled woman', used in section 7. The leader of the synagogue and the crowd in that story were denounced by Jesus as hypocrites because they put their own religious scruples about keeping the Sabbath ahead of any concern for the woman herself. They did not even show the sort of concessions that they would readily make for their domestic animals on the Sabbath. In story after story compassion does seem to trump everything else, even strongly held and principled scruples.

Surely we should be offering such compassion to the terminally ill who are begging to be released from an agonizing death?

If I could be persuaded that other vulnerable people would be unaffected by a change in the law, I would readily respond 'yes' to this question. Paul Badham's challenge is a very real one, especially for those who see compassion as crucial and central.

Of course there is an ongoing debate within palliative medicine itself about whether or not there really is intractable pain or agony, and I am not remotely qualified to make any judgement. Further, in many instances, as experienced hospital visitors will know, it is the understandable agony of the relatives of a terminally ill patient that is most insistent. 'Something must be done, doctor,' is the demand that every general practitioner will have heard repeatedly.

Yet, as I write, more than one hundred terminally ill people have gone to clinics in Switzerland where assisted suicide is legal. So far the Director of Public Prosecutions has decided not to prosecute any of the relatives who have aided and abetted them (even though their action is arguably contrary to the 1961 Suicide Act). In every instance the Director has acted compassionately, believing that such prosecutions would neither serve any public purpose nor be supported by any jury if they came to trial.

As a result there is now a very delicate balance. Relatives who behave compassionately, even while very possibly acting in a way contrary to the Suicide Act, have been treated compassionately by the legal authorities. Yet these authorities still retain the power in law to prosecute any families who act coercively. The result may not be particularly tidy in legal terms. But it is driven throughout by compassion.

Readers will still differ about whether or not the law could be changed safely. Some will agree with Paul Badham that it is possible to put effective legal safeguards into place in order to avoid abuse and to ensure that the elderly and vulnerable are adequately protected. Others, like me, will fear that a change in law might put elderly and vulnerable people (many of whom already feel that they are a burden to their families) under further pressure, damage doctor–patient relationships, and open the way to involuntary euthanasia.

Compassion does not resolve this particular debate. Yet it is crucial and central to both of these positions.

MEDITATION

Psalm 46.1–3

God is our refuge and strength,
a very present help in trouble.
Therefore we will not fear, though the earth should change,
though the mountains shake in the heart of the sea;
though its waters roar and foam,
though the mountains tremble with its tumult.

Sura 55.25

All that dwells upon the earth is perishing, yet still abides the Face of your LORD, majestic splendid. Of which of your LORD 's bounties will you and you deny? Whatsoever is in the heavens and the earth implore him; every day he is upon some labour.

17

The Policeman's Dilemma

Five years ago I served on a panel of religious representatives giving evidence to a Select Committee on Assisted Dying. One of the committee members asked us all to respond to the following story:

> An armed policeman chanced upon a bad road accident in which a truck had caught fire. The truck driver was trapped in his cab and could not escape. As the flames started to reach his cab he shouted out for help but no one could get anywhere near because of the intense heat of the fire. The cab started to burn. He was in agony and cried out to the policeman: 'Please, please shoot me, I am going to die anyway!' Should the policeman have shot or should he just have watched as the truck driver slowly burned to death?

The implications of the story were obvious. Watching someone dying in agony without doing anything effective to end that agony is like watching the poor truck driver burn to death instead of shooting him.

Unbeknown to our panel this committee member had put this classic Policeman's Dilemma to several previous witnesses. Now it was our turn to respond. Another committee member, strongly opposed to legalizing assisted dying, quickly pointed out the fictional nature of the story. Firing a gun when petrol was spilling over the road from the accident was hardly to be recommended. Yet the point of the story was obvious to all of us. So we did respond.

Some panel members argued that human life was sacred, so it would always be wrong to shoot even in these extraordinary circumstances. I prefer instead to talk about human life being God-given rather than sacred, since we value it strongly but we do not actually worship it. As a gift from God we should always be grateful for and value human life, but unless this is a coercive gift and thus not a gift of love it cannot bind us for ever. In any case, unless someone is committed to a strictly pacifist position there are occasions when, however mournfully, human life is legitimately taken.

Some were shocked by my response to the dilemma: Of course the policeman should act compassionately and shoot the truck driver. Yet no one should then frame a law that allowed policemen to shoot anyone who requested this. It is one thing for an individual to act compassionately despite principled (even legal) objections. It is quite another for society to legalize such spontaneous actions. Perhaps difficult cases really do make bad laws.

This response derived from my understanding of the most distinctive feature of Jesus' ethical teaching. Through the parables and healing stories runs a challenging claim: compassion can trump even the most principled scruples. As we shall be seeing in the next chapter, time and again Jesus seemed to defy the strongest conventions of his contemporaries in the interests of compassion. He touched and was touched by those deemed to be deeply and dangerously impure but who came to him asking for compassion. He healed repeatedly on the Sabbath and ate with social outcasts.

In Mark the stories of the feeding of both the four thousand and the five thousand are premised upon 'compassion' (again that visceral Greek word):

As he went ashore, he saw a great crowd; and he had compassion for them, because they were like sheep without a shepherd; and he began to teach them many things. When it grew late, his disciples came to him and said, 'This is a deserted place, and the hour is now very late; send them away so that they may go into the surrounding country and villages and buy something for themselves to eat.' But he answered them, 'You give them something to eat.' (6.34–37)

In those days when there was again a great crowd without anything to eat, he called his disciples and said to them, 'I have compassion for the crowd, because they have been with me now for three days and have nothing to eat. If I send them away hungry to their homes, they will faint on the way – and some of them have come from a great distance.' (8.1–3)

Compassion does appear to be important in the Gospels.

———◆———

MEDITATION

Psalm 136.1

O give thanks to the LORD, for he is good,
for his steadfast love endures for ever.

Sura 34.1

Praise belongs to God to whom belongs whatsoever is in the earth
. . . He is the All-wise, the All-aware . . . the All-compassionate,
the All-forgiving.

18

Compassion and God

If God is seen as wholly compassionate, we in turn should have compassion for each other and for the world that God has entrusted to us. Compassion should be central for us as human beings because God is already compassionate towards us.

This very important belief is shared alike by Jews, Christians, Muslims and people of many different religious faiths. It gives religious people a particularly strong reason for caring for each other and for the world entrusted to them. All is God-given and not simply fortuitous and should be approached with gratitude, respect and humility. It is one of the most significant social differences between those with religious faith and those without.

Sir Jonathan Sacks, the Chief Rabbi, has argued that, seen in terms of evolution, religion offers a bridge between selfish individuals and cooperative societies. Modern understandings of evolution (which he, along with most other religious leaders today, fully accepts) tend to suggest that the so-called survival of the fittest inclines individuals to be selfish (sometimes identified as the 'selfish gene') but also favours societies in which individuals cooperate with each other. It is not at all obvious how to reconcile the tension between the two. However, most religions are adept at attempting to do just that, encouraging otherwise selfish individuals to move beyond self and to be compassionate to each other and indeed to the world at large. Without the strong shared convictions of religion it is not apparent how this cooperation is to be fostered.

Yet there is an obvious problem. The examples of extreme human suffering cited earlier by Paul Badham are difficult to reconcile with a belief that God is wholly compassionate. Some people, like Charles Darwin himself who lost a beloved daughter and then lost his religious faith, conclude that there might be no God after all. Innocent suffering and a wholly compassionate God appear to be considerably at odds with each other.

Not all suffering, of course, is innocent. Human beings have a terrible tendency (the selfish gene again) to inflict deep suffering upon each other. Unless God is to intervene each time this happens and thus obliterate free-will such suffering does seem to be inevitable. Again, pain does have a positive function. It warns living creatures when their bodies are in danger.

Christians also believe that God knows our suffering from within. Jesus, suffering and dying on a cross, shares it with us. This is no distant God, but a compassionate (literally 'suffering alongside') God.

Yet there is still a deep problem. If God is all-powerful, all-knowing and wholly compassionate, why is so much innocent suffering allowed? Why did God not create the universe without such suffering or just with considerably less suffering? Surely this was possible?

Was it really possible? Suppose for a moment that this is the only way that the universe could have been created if it were to generate self-conscious, moral life. Perhaps it could have been created in no other way. Physical changes, sometimes in the form of destructive volcanoes and tsunamis, and genetic mutations, sometimes resulting in deadly viruses, are simply part and parcel of a world that generates moral life.

Things could not have been otherwise. Human beings may be very clever but do they *really* know how the universe could have been created differently?

Some reach this stage in the argument but then point out that God might have concluded that it would have been better to have had no universe in the first place than to have created one in which innocent suffering was inevitable. Better nothing than anything that results in innocent suffering.

Yet in practice that is not what most of us eventually conclude. Paul Badham's examples are fortunately the exception rather than the rule. Most of us conclude that life really is worth living despite innocent suffering. We may conclude differently in the final stages of our life if palliative care really is unable to help us. However, for most of our lives we do want to live despite human suffering, and we grieve rather than rejoice when those we love die young.

In our everyday lives, then, we do seem to be reconciled to innocent suffering, even if we are sometimes puzzled by it. We choose to live, and want others to live, unless personal suffering becomes quite overwhelming.

In short, most of us conclude that life is good rather than evil. And this conclusion is indeed compatible with a conviction that compassion should be central for us as human beings because God is already compassionate towards us.

———➤●◄———

MEDITATION

Psalm 100.5

For the LORD is good;
his steadfast love endures for ever,
and his faithfulness to all generations.

Sura 35.35

God knows the Unseen in the heavens and the earth; he knows the thoughts within the breasts. It is he who appointed you viceroys in the earth.

WEEK 4

Care

———⟫●⟪———

19

The story of the Caring Samaritan

Just then a lawyer stood up to test Jesus. 'Teacher,' he said, 'what must I do to inherit eternal life?' He said to him, 'What is written in the law? What do you read there?' He answered, 'You shall love the Lord your God with all your heart, and with all your soul, and with all your strength, and with all your mind; and your neighbour as yourself.' And he said to him, 'You have given the right answer; do this, and you will live.'

But wanting to justify himself, he asked Jesus, 'And who is my neighbour?' Jesus replied, 'A man was going down from Jerusalem to Jericho, and fell into the hands of robbers, who stripped him, beat him, and went away, leaving him half dead. Now by chance a priest was going down that road; and when he saw him, he passed by on the other side. So likewise a Levite, when he came to the place and saw him, passed by on the other side. But a Samaritan while travelling came near him; and when he saw him, he was moved with pity. He went to him and bandaged his wounds, having poured oil and wine on them. Then he put him on his own animal, brought him to an inn, and took care of him. The next day he took out two denarii, gave them to the innkeeper, and said, "Take care of him; and when I come back, I will repay you whatever more you spend." Which of these three, do you think, was a neighbour to the man who fell into the hands of the robbers?' He said, 'The one who showed him mercy.' Jesus said to him, 'Go and do likewise.' (Luke 10.25–37)

As already seen, this celebrated parable is told only in Luke, where it is introduced with an explanation that it exemplifies the two commandments, to love God and to love neighbour. It also helps to unpack further the conviction that compassion should be central for us as human beings because God is already compassionate towards us.

Curiously, in Mark and Matthew it is Jesus rather than the lawyer who brings these two Jewish commandments together (in the Old Testament they are separated). There has been much debate among scholars about whether or not this combination of the two commandments originated with or (as Luke might suggest) predated Jesus. It may not matter too much. Christians have long seen this combination as exemplifying the teaching of Jesus, whether he was using older ideas or not. In turn this much-loved parable exemplifies the commandments.

As in the Parable of the Prodigal, 'compassion' appears at a pivotal moment in the story. The translation here, that the Samaritan 'was moved with pity', rather hides this important point. The Greek word used in both parables is indeed the visceral word for 'compassion'. Both might be read as stories about the centrality of compassion and both contain other less than compassionate figures. According to this interpretation, in the Prodigal it is the elder brother who failed to show compassion, here it is the priest and the Levite (key figures in Temple worship at Jerusalem). In the Prodigal it is the father, despite having been treated so truculently, who was compassionate, here it is the outsider, a Samaritan (a member of a neighbouring and often hated people who regarded only Mount Gerizim as the proper place for worship).

However, the Samaritan story also exemplifies extensive care. Note the way that the Samaritan . . .

- went to him
- bandaged his wounds
- poured oil and wine on them
- put him on his own animal
- brought him to an inn
- took care of him
- gave two denarii to the innkeeper
- said, 'Take care of him'
- and 'I will repay you whatever more you spend.'

Altogether a fairly comprehensive package of care. Not of course that all of these specific actions would be recommended today. Oil and wine in the wounds, transport on an animal and care in an inn would not normally be considered appropriate today. And the Samaritan might have campaigned to make the road to Jericho safer for other travellers!

More seriously (and less literally) this story combines compassion and care, or, if you prefer, ethics and care provision. The Samaritan did not just reach out to a vulnerable person in urgent need of help, he made immediate and practical provisions to ensure that help really was given. In contrast, the two religious figureheads 'passed by on the other side'.

It was the outsider alone who exemplified compassionate care.

───➤●◄───

MEDITATION

Psalm 147.2–3

The LORD . . . gathers the outcasts of Israel.
He heals the broken-hearted, and binds up their wounds.

Sura 2.100

Know you not that to God belongs the kingdom of the heavens and the earth, and that you have none, apart from God, neither protector nor helper?

20

The founder of the Samaritans

Chad Varah, Rector of St Stephen, Walbrook and founder of the Samaritans, died aged 95 on 8 November 2007. The very next day *The Times* published a full-page obituary. There cannot be many Anglican clergy, other than archbishops, who might receive such an accolade. It began:

> It was as the leader and inspirer of the Samaritans, founded to befriend the suicidal and despairing, that Chad Varah's name became known worldwide. The idea of the organisation, which came to him in his forties, transformed his life. He brought to the task not just a strong personality and a natural compassion but also a firm grasp on the value of publicity combined with a gift for showmanship.

Chad Varah was a highly unconventional Anglican priest. He was ordained (after struggling with last-minute doubts) in 1935 and finally retired as Rector of St Stephen's aged 92. By then he was the oldest serving incumbent in the Church of England (he was appointed before a retirement age was introduced) and was walking with the aid of a Zimmer frame. Despite being ordained he was a firm believer in reincarnation, entitling his autobiography *Before I Die Again*. The obituary depicted the latter as 'a curiously ill-disciplined and self-regarding work'. Humility may not have been one of his more consistent merits.

Nor seemingly was tact. Objecting to Pope John Paul II's views on contraception, he wrote in the *Sunday Telegraph* in 1993 that 'It was a great mistake to make an ignorant Polish peasant into a Pope.' He apparently told *Penthouse* magazine that he would rather his daughter became a prostitute than a policewoman. And even in his final sermon before retiring he caused controversy, using it to defend the appointment of a gay bishop.

Like the Samaritan in the parable he was forever an outsider. He also exemplified compassionate care in a manner that was indeed a bit like Jesus.

Beneath his 'gift for showmanship' was something much more profound: a deep compassion and a drive to care passionately. His life-long ministry was concerned with vulnerable people in suicidal despair. In the aftermath of Victorian England he came very early to the conclusion that many young people were driven to despair and even suicide because of ignorance about sex. This led him to believe that a non-judgemental, compassionate approach was essential to good counselling. Again from the *Times* obituary:

> From his earliest days as a curate he specialised in counselling on sexual problems and wrote articles on the subject from a permissive point of view, refusing to condemn adultery in all circumstances, and maintaining that the only law was the law of love . . . When he heard, while at Clapham, that there were three suicides a day in London, it seemed to him that God was calling him to extend his counselling to those contemplating taking their own lives. But it was only when he was appointed to the exquisite City church of St Stephen, Walbrook (regarded as Wren's template for St Paul's, with central dome) that he was able to put his ideas into practice. On November 1, 1953, he announced his plans for what was to be a life-long commitment, originally called The Good Samaritans.

So he set up his famous emergency telephone helpline and organized volunteers to be experts in 'listening therapy', making it a strict rule that no Samaritan should attempt to convert those who called to any religion or philosophy. Nor were they to be judgemental in any way about sexual issues. They were simply to listen sympathetically. Ironically, the result, as the obituary notes, was that 'an ordained minister, operating from the crypt of a famous church, founded a wholly secular personal rescue service'.

Yet his unconventional and idiosyncratic personality eventually proved to be too much even for the charity that he had founded. By 1973, aged 63, he had been removed as director of the Samaritans' Central London branch. He was appointed a Companion of Honour for services to the Samaritans in 2000, but it was not until 2005 that a full rapprochement with the charity was finally made.

Undeterred, on leaving the London Samaritans he launched instead Befrienders International. And, since St Stephen's was closed for nine years while it was undergoing structural repairs, he then travelled round and round the world inspiring others to do similar voluntary work in their own countries.

If compassion properly understood involves a threefold response – identifying someone as being in real need, feeling strongly for that person, and then being determined to help that person in any way possible – then surely Chad Varah must count as being more compassionate than most other people. He had a strong commitment and determination to care over many decades. Few other carers have been quite so dedicated and single-minded.

Manifestly he had quirks and foibles. Yet his compassionate care for those at their most vulnerable and desperate does indeed seem to be a bit like Jesus.

⸻➤●◄⸻

MEDITATION

Psalm 72.13–14

He has pity on the weak and the needy,
and saves the lives of the needy.
From oppression and violence he redeems their life;
and precious is their blood in his sight.

Sura 4.130

O believers, be you securers of justice, witnesses to God,
even though it be against yourselves, or your parents and kinsmen,
whether the man be rich or poor.

21

Care for the leper

A leper came to him begging him, and kneeling he said to him, 'If you choose, you can make me clean.' Moved with pity, Jesus stretched out his hand and touched him, and said to him, 'I do choose. Be made clean!' Immediately the leprosy left him, and he was made clean. After sternly warning him he sent him away at once, saying to him, 'See that you say nothing to anyone; but go, show yourself to the priest, and offer for your cleansing what Moses commanded, as a testimony to them.' But he went out and began to proclaim it freely, and to spread the word, so that Jesus could no longer go into a town openly, but stayed out in the country; and people came to him from every quarter. (Mark 1.40–45)

The Samaritan made immediate and practical provisions to make sure that help really was given to the unfortunate victim on the road to Jericho. Such practical help is indeed part of care. Chad Varah was also well aware of that. Yet there is much more to good care.

Rather unusually, someone who was working as a care assistant came to study for a master's degree. He had chosen to be a care assistant despite already being a graduate. Teaching him was a real privilege. From him I began to understand the difference between professional codes of practice (good governance) and care properly understood. He argued that if he stuck rigidly to the professional code for care assistants and did nothing beyond this, his work in reality would be less than caring. Little acts of kindness, friendship and compassion, that cannot readily be codified, would be absent. The vulnerable and dependent people in his care would receive scrupulously methodical attention but not the person-to-person care that actually makes their lives worth living. Care in this fuller sense requires care for and about the one who is vulnerable.

That is what Mark's story of the 'leper' illustrates so well. Once more Jesus was 'moved with pity' (the Greek here in some texts is again that visceral word for 'compassion') and responded to the one who 'came to him begging him, and kneeling'. Here was someone vulnerable and desperate. Yet Jesus' actions went further. He acted with real passion and actually touched him despite his 'leprosy'. Luke heightens the story. This was not just 'a leper' but 'a man covered with leprosy'.

Except that it almost certainly was not 'leprosy' in the modern sense at all. True leprosy, or Hansen's disease, has a number of identifying features: areas of skin that lose all feeling, painless and progressive ulceration of fingers or toes, and facial nodules. Not one of these features is mentioned anywhere in the Bible in connection with 'leprosy'. In the extended depictions of 'leprosy' in Leviticus some quite different skin condition or conditions are noted instead:

> The priest shall examine the disease on the skin of his body, and if the hair in the diseased area has turned white and the disease appears to be deeper than the skin of his body, it is a leprous disease . . . When a man or a woman has spots on the skin of the body, white spots, the priest shall make an examination, and if the spots on the skin of the body are of a dull white, it is a rash that has broken out on the skin; he is clean. If anyone loses the hair from his head, he is bald but he is clean. If he loses the hair from his forehead and temples, he has baldness of the forehead but he is clean. But if there is on the bald head or the bald forehead a reddish-white diseased spot, it is a leprous disease breaking out on his bald head or his bald forehead. The priest shall examine him; if the diseased swelling is reddish-white on his bald head or on his bald forehead, which resembles a leprous disease in the skin of the body, he is leprous, he is unclean. The priest shall pronounce

him unclean; the disease is on his head. The person who has the leprous disease shall wear torn clothes and let the hair of his head be dishevelled; and he shall cover his upper lip and cry out, 'Unclean, unclean.' He shall remain unclean as long as he has the disease; he is unclean. He shall live alone; his dwelling shall be outside the camp. (Leviticus 13.3, 38–46)

I find it quite difficult to read this passage without scratching!

Even though some of the skin conditions depicted here might have been relatively harmless, they were clearly much feared in the ancient world. Those affected were subject to strict social exclusion until they had been pronounced 'clean' by the priest. Even King Uzziah 'being leprous lived in a separate house, for he was excluded from the house of the Lord' (2 Chronicles 26.21). While 'lepers' had their condition they were regarded as deeply impure. They could make their family impure, their house impure, the whole community impure and (most disastrously of all) the Temple itself impure.

Yet Jesus touched the 'leper'.

———⋙●⋘———

MEDITATION

Psalm 121.8

The LORD will keep
your going out and your coming in
from this time on and for evermore.

Sura 11.75

The mercy of God and his blessings be upon you.

22

Touching the stigmatized

Many have found an important precedent here for how we should care properly for those with AIDS. As seen in section 10, some early responses to AIDS were inept and even hypocritical. Today many religious agencies working among those living with AIDS are thankfully quite different. Listening to better informed medical science and reading their Bibles more carefully, many Christians working in this area have come to realize that the early responses were not a bit like Jesus. The story of Jesus touching the 'leper' has been used again and again to encourage this radical change. If Jesus did this, then we can touch and care for those living with AIDS today.

Compare Jesus' action in the Gospels with that of Elisha in the Old Testament. Luke explicitly notes this comparison. In his pivotal story of Jesus speaking in the synagogue (the foundation story for Liberation Theology in Latin America), Jesus declares: 'There were also many lepers in Israel in the time of the prophet Elisha, and none of them was cleansed except Naaman' (Luke 4.27). And both Luke and Matthew recount how Jesus told John the Baptist's disciples: 'Go and tell John what you have seen and heard: the blind receive their sight, the lame walk, the lepers are cleansed, the deaf hear, the dead are raised, the poor have good news brought to them' (Luke 7.22).

In the Old Testament story, Naaman, the great commander of the army of the King of Aram, 'though a mighty warrior, suffered from leprosy'. Hearing about the healing powers of the prophet Elisha, he came to him laden with rich rewards:

Naaman came with his horses and chariots, and halted at the entrance of Elisha's house. Elisha sent a messenger to him, saying, 'Go, wash in the Jordan seven times, and your flesh shall be restored and you shall be clean.' But Naaman became angry and went away, saying, 'I thought that for me he would surely come out, and stand and call on the name of the LORD his God, and would wave his hand over the spot, and cure the leprosy! Are not Abana and Pharpar, the rivers of Damascus, better than all the waters of Israel? Could I not wash in them, and be clean?' He turned and went away in a rage. But his servants approached and said to him, 'Father, if the prophet had commanded you to do something difficult, would you not have done it? How much more, when all he said to you was, "Wash, and be clean"?' So he went down and immersed himself seven times in the Jordan, according to the word of the man of God; his flesh was restored like the flesh of a young boy, and he was clean. (2 Kings 5.9–14)

In Mark's story a 'leper' also comes to Jesus seeking healing. A ritual is prescribed: 'Go, show yourself to the priest, and offer for your cleansing what Moses commanded.' And 'the leprosy left him, and he was made clean'. But there is also a crucial difference. Elisha avoided meeting the 'leper' before he had been cleansed and simply sent a message out to him, whereas Jesus 'stretched out his hand and touched him'.

The detailed instructions in Leviticus about how the priest should inspect those feared to have 'leprosy' never mentioned touching. If the person did have 'leprosy' and the priest had touched that person, then the priest himself would have been rendered ritually impure. Such dangerous impurity was regarded as highly contagious. Impurity is not be confused with modern concepts of germs and viruses. It was considered to be much more serious than that. Impurity endangered a person's relationship to God, and only ritual sacrifices could restore that relationship. Disastrously, impurity put holiness at serious risk – even the holiness of the Temple itself.

There is a parallel here with modern India, especially in rural areas where the ritual caste system survives. The Dalit community still tends to be stigmatized as an 'outcast' community of 'untouchables'. Many non-Dalits refuse to do work regarded as 'impure', such as handling dead bodies or human excrement, and leave this for Dalits to do instead. Even the nursing profession is affected by these notions of impurity. So, despite the fact that Christians in India represent just 2 per cent of the total population, nurses tend to be disproportionately drawn from Christian families. They are not quite so subject as others to qualms about impurity, having been nurtured on stories about Jesus touching those deemed to be impure and of him eating with outcasts.

A major part of the work of UNAIDS over the last few years has been to challenge stigmatization. Of course, at a scientific level leprosy (even in the biblical sense) and AIDS are quite different diseases. Yet at a social level they have features in common. So, many stigmatizing, misleading and similar responses have been targeted at both groups of people: about their dangerous and contagious impurity, about their sinful behaviour, about the need for them to be socially excluded. UNAIDS argues that if such stigmatization could be eliminated, those living with HIV would come forward for testing and treatment and could then be encouraged to behave in ways that do not transfer the virus to others.

By cuddling a child living with AIDS the late Princess Diana admirably demonstrated how such stigmatization might be broken down.

By touching a deeply stigmatized man it was indeed Jesus who showed just how all of us should respond to people stigmatized today.

⟩⟩●⟨⟨

MEDITATION

Psalm 146.7–9

The LORD sets the prisoners free;
the LORD opens the eyes of the blind.
The LORD lifts up those who are bowed down;
the LORD loves the righteous.
The LORD watches over the strangers.

Sura 24.60

There is no fault in the blind, and there is no fault in the lame,
and there is no fault in the sick.

23

Care of the dying

Soon afterwards he went to a town called Nain, and his disciples and a large crowd went with him. As he approached the gate of the town, a man who had died was being carried out. He was his mother's only son, and she was a widow; and with her was a large crowd from the town. When the Lord saw her, he had compassion for her and said to her, 'Do not weep.' Then he came forward and touched the bier, and the bearers stood still. And he said, 'Young man, I say to you, rise!' The dead man sat up and began to speak, and Jesus gave him to his mother. Fear seized all of them; and they glorified God, saying, 'A great prophet has risen among us!' and 'God has looked favourably on his people!' This word about him spread throughout Judea and all the surrounding country. (Luke 7.11–17)

In the interests of compassionate care Jesus risked dangerous impurity from both the dead and the living. Luke's story of the Widow's Son at Nain once again uses the visceral word for compassion, as this translation suggests. As Jesus, his disciples and a large crowd approached the town gate they were met by another large crowd moving in the opposite direction. The two crowds intersected. When Jesus spotted the dead man's mother, herself a widow, 'he had compassion for her and said to her, "Do not weep."' Then, putting himself at risk of impurity, he 'came forward and touched the bier'. And 'the bearers stood still', as well they might, in astonishment perhaps. Luke writes tersely that 'the dead man sat up and began to speak, and Jesus gave him to his mother'. Unsurprisingly 'fear seized all of them'.

There are echoes of older stories from both classical sources and the Old Testament in the telling of this story. An allusion is made to the prophet Elijah since it was told that he also raised a widow's son (although 1 Kings 17 tells that story much more elaborately than Luke does his). A similar story is also recounted in the classical writings of Philostratus. However, the emphasis upon compassionate care is specific to Luke. Here Jesus cared passionately for and about the plight of the widow.

Compassionate care for the dying and their relatives was the hallmark of another remarkable Anglican, who died aged 87 in 2005, Dame Cicely Saunders. Studying on a course for those interested in hospital ministry in the late 1960s I was fortunate to hear her speak when she was still in the early days of developing the hospice movement. Some of the occasional frailties of this movement and of palliative care in general have already been noticed in section 16. Paul Badham focused upon these in his defence of assisted suicide. These occasional frailties (if that is what they are) should not overshadow the astonishing achievements of both the hospice movement and palliative care.

After a somewhat frustrating experience as a nurse, Cicely Saunders trained in middle life to become a doctor in order to bring a higher standard of medicine and care to those who were dying. As a result of her training, faith and compassionate care she was instrumental in developing modern hospices which have been a source of comfort and help to many dying people. They have brought relief to countless relatives struggling to cope with the one that they loved dying, and have helped many people near death themselves to come to terms with the process of dying.

The *Times* obituary for her began:

Dame Cicely Saunders earned gratitude, admiration and international renown for helping to alleviate the suffering of terminally ill people. Hundreds of hospices in Britain and more than 95 other countries are modelled on St Christopher's, Sydenham, the hospice which she established in 1967. St Christopher's, on her initiative, attempted for the first time to provide patient-centred palliative care for the terminally ill, combining emotional, spiritual and social support with expert medical and nursing care. Its practices have since been widely copied and developed. Today St Christopher's cares for about 2,000 patients and their families each year and, in training more than 60,000 health professionals, has influenced standards of care for the dying throughout the world.

Palliative care medicine is now widely practised beyond hospices and has helped doctors to use dangerous, pain-relieving drugs more effectively and responsibly. Many people imagine that doctors regularly give the terminally ill large doses of these drugs in order deliberately to shorten their lives – unofficial euthanasia, if you will. Whether or not this happened much in the past, it is less likely today. Most doctors no longer work in isolation, and other members of a health-care team can now challenge such unofficial euthanasia if it happens.

The reality is probably much nearer to the British Medical Association's position, namely that these drugs should be given to patients only in proportion to their pain and discomfort, even if this does entail giving what would otherwise be quite large amounts (which patients in pain appear often to tolerate). Conversely, life-sustaining treatment is only withdrawn or withheld when it ceases to have any medical benefit for a patient, or when a conscious patient demands that it must be withdrawn or withheld. The palliative care movement has been a significant agent in helping the medical profession today to make such crucial distinctions.

Again the *Times* obituary for Cicely Saunders captures her achievement in palliative care:

Her experience as a volunteer in St Luke's, the Bayswater Home for the Dying Poor, persuaded Saunders to challenge the received medical wisdom about dying, death and bereavement . . . She then combined membership of a research group on pain, set up at St Mary's, Paddington, with her continuing

ward work – this time at St Joseph's Hackney, where the
Sisters of Charity showed her how much might be done for
the dying by sustained loving care; and where she, in turn,
began to bring into play her more unorthodox ideas about
pain relief. What she then demonstrated, and what is now
widely adopted, was that intermittent reactive sedation of
surging pain was far less effective than achieving a steady
state in which the dying patient could still maintain con-
sciousness and even life with some quality.

Like Chad Varah she worked relentlessly over many years to
put in place a structure of care that could realize her vision:

It took years of planning and financing to open a purpose-
built hospice on the Sydenham site. There Saunders explored
all the possibilities for matching quality medical care with
support for patients and their families at home, changing
existing medical and social attitudes about the care of the
dying. Through the struggles for financial and professional
backing, in which Saunders proved herself as a medical director, a fundraiser of quiet genius, a relentless administrator and
a proponent of the hospice idea on the world stage, it was
clear that she was achieving exactly what she set out to do.

(*The Times*, 15 July 2005)

———————

MEDITATION

Psalm 113.7

He raises the poor from the dust,
and lifts the needy from the ash heap.

Sura 24.60

Why, surely to God belongs whatsoever is in the heavens and the
earth; He ever knows what state you are upon.

24

Moral passion

There is one feature common to these different examples of care. It is passion. Care is not seen as just a part of one's job, something that can be codified, or (even worse) as an arbitrary life-style choice. This is *passionate* care, driving remarkable people such as Chad Varah and Cicely Saunders to devote their whole lives to it.

Passion is evident in many of the stories about Jesus and in some of those that he told himself. Mark's story of the 'leper' contains the sentence: 'After sternly warning him [Jesus] sent him away at once.' The Greek word used here for 'sternly warning' is full of passion. In ancient Greek it was sometimes used to denote the snorting of a horse. Some have suggested that a more passionate translation of the sentence here is: 'Moved by deep feeling towards him, immediately he drove him forth.' Jesus was passionately concerned for this man and for his welfare.

We have already noted considerable passion in Jesus' charge of 'hypocrisy' directed at those who were religiously active and their leaders. The language here is sharp and deliberately offensive. As it is in the following story:

Again he entered the synagogue, and a man was there who had a withered hand. They watched him to see whether he would cure him on the sabbath, so that they might accuse him. And he said to the man who had the withered hand, 'Come forward.' Then he said to them, 'Is it lawful to do good or to do harm on the sabbath, to save life or to kill?' But they were silent. He looked around at them with anger; he was grieved at their hardness of heart and said to the man, 'Stretch out your hand.' He stretched it out, and his hand was restored. The Pharisees went out and immediately conspired with the Herodians against him, how to destroy him. (Mark 3.1–6)

So offensive indeed that his religious critics 'immediately conspired . . . how to destroy him'. Jesus had once more broken the
Sabbath in order to heal someone and had brusquely challenged
his critics. Challenging action and challenging words.

There is also the deliberate irony noted earlier that Jesus
deployed in some of his parables. For example, comparing hypocritical behaviour with failing to notice a whole log stuck in the
hypocrite's eye. Or portraying the fate of the bemused goats in
the lurid terms of eternal punishment.

And of course there is the driving out of the sellers from the
Temple, which has sometimes been used as a justification for
muscular Christianity. John places this at the beginning of Jesus'
ministry and treats it as a symbolic event, a sort of acted parable.
In contrast, the earlier three Gospels place it towards the end.
There is much dispute among scholars about the significance of
this difference. For some, placing it towards the end of Jesus' ministry deliberately links it to the Passion story, suggesting that the
attack on the Temple was a trigger for Jesus' arrest. Others are
not so convinced, arguing that one man would hardly have been
able to drive out those who were selling and those who were
buying (as Mark insists), nor be able to prohibit 'anyone to carry
anything through the temple', let alone dispel them for good.

Whatever the significance of this sharp event, Jesus' moral
passion in the story is obvious:

> [Jesus] was teaching and saying, 'Is it not written,
>> "My house shall be called a house of prayer for all the
>> nations"?
> But you have made it a den of robbers.'
> And when the chief priests and the scribes heard it, they kept
> looking for a way to kill him. (Mark 11.17–18)

Care in this sense is quite clearly not just some life-style choice.
This is passionate care. It involves a deep conviction that things
are wrong and need to be changed.

It is sometimes claimed that values are purely subjective.
We make our own values and arbitrarily choose to follow some

subjective values rather than others. Ethics is simply a matter of taste or custom. For many ancient Greeks the word 'ethics' simply meant that. Similarly for many ancient Romans 'morality' was just that. An arbitrary custom or a matter of taste: that and nothing more.

After 9/11 there is some wisdom here. People can have passionate convictions about issues that strike most others as being highly subjective. For example, people can feel morally outraged about the length of others' hair or their style of dress. More dangerously, they can become convinced that God commands them to murder other people. Even deeply and sincerely held religious convictions can be profoundly misguided and dangerous.

Yet the moral passion in Jesus' actions and responses in the Gospels points to something else. Passionate care, properly directed, seems to be an essential component of his ministry and to derive from a conviction that some things really *are* wrong. His denunciation of hypocrites on several occasions was a denunciation of those who pretended to be compassionate or holy when they manifestly were not. Their action and words were seen as an affront to God.

The passionate belief in God in the Gospels carries with it a conviction about the reality of good. Compassionate care is not simply and entirely invented *by* us. Properly understood it is grounded in God's compassionate care *for* us.

———⟫●⟪———

MEDITATION

Psalm 82.3

Give justice to the weak and the orphan;
maintain the right of the lowly and the destitute.

Sura 4.1

Give the orphans their property, and do not exchange the corrupt for the good; and devour not their property with your property; surely that is a great crime.

WEEK 5

Faith

———>●<———

25

Your faith has made you well

And a large crowd followed him and pressed in on him. Now there was a woman who had been suffering from haemorrhages for twelve years. She had endured much under many physicians, and had spent all that she had; and she was no better, but rather grew worse. She had heard about Jesus, and came up behind him in the crowd and touched his cloak, for she said, 'If I but touch his clothes, I will be made well.' Immediately her haemorrhage stopped; and she felt in her body that she was healed of her disease. Immediately aware that power had gone forth from him, Jesus turned about in the crowd and said, 'Who touched my clothes?' And his disciples said to him, 'You see the crowd pressing in on you; how can you say, "Who touched me?"' He looked all round to see who had done it. But the woman, knowing what had happened to her, came in fear and trembling, fell down before him, and told him the whole truth. He said to her, 'Daughter, your faith has made you well; go in peace, and be healed of your disease.' (Mark 5.25–34)

This is one of the most heartfelt healing stories in Mark. Matthew and Luke both tell the same story but omit many of Mark's finer details. And all three sandwich the story within that of Jairus' daughter. It is a story within a story.

It is also one of three different stories in these Gospels that conclude with the words, 'your faith has made you well', 'your faith has saved you', or 'your faith has made you whole' (depending upon how the Greek verb is translated).

A strong reference by Jesus to faith is a feature of many healing stories in the Gospels. In quite a number faith appears to be an essential requirement of healing. Conversely, a lack of faith is given as a reason for Jesus being unable to act:

> He came to his home town and began to teach the people in their synagogue, so that they were astounded and said, 'Where did this man get this wisdom and these deeds of power? Is not this the carpenter's son? Is not his mother called Mary? And are not his brothers James and Joseph and Simon and Judas? And are not all his sisters with us? Where then did this man get all this?' And they took offence at him. But Jesus said to them, 'Prophets are not without honour except in their own country and in their own house.' And he did not do many deeds of power there, because of their unbelief. (Matthew 13.54–58)

In Mark's earlier version of this story a lack of faith or trust among the people of Jesus' home town is noted. Matthew strengthens this and unambiguously makes this lack of faith the reason why Jesus was unable to do 'many deeds of power there'. Faith or trust is clearly regarded as pretty crucial and perhaps even essential for healing.

Mark's story of the woman 'suffering from haemorrhages' is manifestly a story about faith or trust: persistent, unnoticed by the disciples, but recognized at once by Jesus, and then rewarded. The details that Mark supplies emphasize her persistence. The woman:

- had been suffering from haemorrhages for twelve years
- had endured much under many physicians
- had spent all that she had
- was no better, but rather grew worse
- had heard about Jesus
- came up behind him in the crowd
- touched his cloak
- and said, 'If I but touch his clothes, I will be made well.'

Persistence indeed.

Jesus then turned about in the crowd and said, 'Who touched my clothes?' And his disciples, quite reasonably, responded, 'You see the crowd pressing in on you; how can you say, "Who touched me?" '

Then Mark adds that the woman, 'knowing what had happened to her, came in fear and trembling, fell down before him, and told him the whole truth'. The story reaches its climax with Jesus' response, 'Daughter, your faith has made you well; go in peace, and be healed of your disease.'

There has been much speculation about the woman's medical condition. For once it is worth noting this speculation. Many have concluded that she had menorrhagia, chronically heavy periods. If so, then this is another healing story involving possible impurity. Contact, even involuntary contact, with menstrual loss would have made Jesus 'unclean'. So, in addition to the impurity from Jesus touching the 'leper' in Mark's first chapter, menstrual impurity (requiring rituals to be removed) might now be added in this fifth chapter (a chapter that also shows Jesus associating with a demoniac and holding a dead girl's hand). Yet Jesus in the story simply ignores this possibility and focuses instead upon the woman's faith.

'Daughter, your faith has made you well.'

MEDITATION

Psalm 116.10

I kept my faith, even when I said,
'I am greatly afflicted' . . .

Sura 8.1

Those only are believers who, when God is mentioned, their hearts
quake, and when his signs are recited to them, it increases them in
faith, and in their LORD they put their trust.

26

Whose faith?

When he returned to Capernaum after some days, it was reported that he was at home. So many gathered around that there was no longer room for them, not even in front of the door; and he was speaking the word to them. Then some people came, bringing to him a paralysed man, carried by four of them. And when they could not bring him to Jesus because of the crowd, they removed the roof above him; and after having dug through it, they let down the mat on which the paralytic lay. When Jesus saw their faith, he said to the paralytic, 'Son, your sins are forgiven.' (Mark 2.1–5)

In most healing stories in the Gospels it is the faith of the one to be healed that Jesus commends. But sometimes it is the faith of parents or friends that is noted. This appears to be just such a story. Of course it is possible that 'their faith' might include that of the paralysed man, although most people read this otherwise. Whichever interpretation is made, Jesus was clearly impressed by the lengths to which the four bearers went, and specifically noted their faith.

While individuals in other stories are praised for their faith, this story suggests that faith can also be shared. A lack of faith can also be shared, as indicated by the people in Jesus' home town. It is all too easy for twenty-first-century Westerners to assume that faith or lack of faith focuses solely upon the state of mind of individuals.

Reading accounts of soldiers who served in the trenches during the First World War suggests that a focus upon individual faith alone is too narrow even in the West. Towards the end of this war a unique survey was undertaken by army chaplains. It offers an extraordinary glimpse of popular religious beliefs at the time.

The Army and Religion, subtitled *An Enquiry and its Bearing upon the Religious Life of the Nation*, was compiled from questionnaires channelled through army chaplains. Altogether some three hundred memoranda were received, 'resting on the evidence of many hundred witnesses . . . from men of all ranks'.

The questionnaire asked, 'What percentage of the men, would you say, are in vital relationship with any of the Churches?' The authors were aware of the ambiguity of the question and of some of the answers received. Nevertheless, they estimated that, whereas four-fifths of the men had been to Sunday school, four-fifths of these did not subsequently go to church as adults. More carefully, they calculated that only about a tenth of the English, a fifth of the Scottish and a third of the Roman Catholic troops were in what they termed 'a vital relationship to a church'.

Despite the general low level of non-Catholic churchgoing, the report maintained that most soldiers believed in God and in prayer. The authors reported poignantly:

> It is very remarkable that the whole materialistic and anti-religious propaganda, which made so much noise, and apparently had so much vogue among our labouring classes a few years ago, seems to have simply withered away in the fires of the Line. The men of the British armies, however dim their faith may be, do in the hour of danger, at least, believe in God, 'the great and terrible God'. Most men we are told pray before they go over the parapet, or advance in the face of machine guns, and they thank God when they have come through the battle . . . [I]n the presence of the most terrific display of material force that human history has ever seen men believe that there is an Unseen Power, inaccessible to the senses, which is yet mightier than high explosives, which knows all and which hears prayer. (D. S. Cairns (ed.), *The Army and Religion*, Macmillan, London, 1919, pp. 7–8)

Linked to these beliefs in God and in prayer was also a general belief in afterlife. Again the report concluded that:

The marked drift of the evidence is that, taken as a whole, the men, though vaguely, believe in the life to come . . . Whatever their present attitude to the Churches may be, they have in them the result of many centuries of Christian training and of the home life that springs up in such a soil. (p. 16)

Nevertheless, the report was not convinced that surrounding beliefs were always specifically Christian. Prefiguring tensions that would sometimes be felt in Remembrance Day services, the report argued: 'The idea of salvation by death in battle for one's country has been widely prevalent, and is one of those points in which the religion of the trenches has rather a Moslem than a Christian colour' (p. 19).

The curious reference to 'Moslem' apart, this remarkable report did seem to point to a shared rather than just an individual faith. Veterans of Afghanistan and Iraq today sometimes report similar experiences. Away from danger many soldiers talk cynically about religious faith of any kind, but faced with imminent death such cynicism can soon evaporate.

Faith shared, however momentarily.

—————➤●◄—————

MEDITATION

Psalm 92.1–2

It is good to give thanks to the LORD,
to sing praises to your name, O Most High;
to declare your steadfast love in the morning,
and your faithfulness by night . . .

Sura 39.35

God is enough for me; in him all those put their trust who put their trust.

27

Faith in Alpha

I cannot claim to read *Alpha News* very often. It can seem too much like propaganda: enthusiastic items about local Alpha groups, which do not always translate into accurate information at local level.

However, just before putting the latest *Alpha News* into the recycling bin, I noticed a small reference on the front page:

One of Britain's hardest criminals says 'My life has totally changed'

I was caught. *Alpha News* explained inside:

For many years, Shane Taylor, 27, was considered to be one of the most dangerous prisoners in Britain's jails. Originally jailed for attempted murder, he had his sentence extended by four years when he attacked a prison officer with a broken glass in an incident which provoked a riot. After that, he was sent to some of Britain's most secure 'Category A' prisons, where he was often held in solitary confinement because of his violence towards prison officers. Then, to his surprise, he found himself on a prison Alpha course. It was the beginning of a new life inside – and now outside – prison. (*Alpha News*, April 2009, p. 5)

Seven months earlier he had described this experience in his own words to Andrew Pain of the *Evening Gazette* as follows:

Prior to me being segregated, I met a fellow prisoner called Robert Bull. This man spoke to me at great length about Jesus

Christ, and I thought he was crazy! However, one thing he said to me stuck in my mind – that he will never get out of prison even though he has served 15 years already [for murder], but in his mind he was already free. At the time I didn't understand what he meant by that, but during my time in segregation I got a clear vision in my mind of Robert Bull the Christian, and an overwhelming urge to write to him. I described how I felt in my letter to him and that the urge to contact him had been completely overpowering, and he replied at once to me. He told me that God was trying to touch my life, he was trying to open my eyes, but that I just didn't know it yet. Again I thought the poor man was indeed crazy. (*Evening Gazette*, 18 September 2008)

Shane Taylor explained to both *Alpha News* and the *Evening Gazette* how this encounter led him first to start reading the Gideon Bible in his isolated cell and then, once out of isolation, to go to a prison Alpha group (although even this he claims to have joined initially for the free tea and biscuits). *Alpha News* continues:

Eventually we got to the Holy Spirit day. After we'd watched the videos and had our discussion everyone sat down and we each got prayed for. The minister put his hand on my head and prayed for me but nothing particularly happened. Later on I was making a cup of coffee when he came up to me and said, 'I've never done this in all the years I've worked here, but I think God is telling me to tell you to come back here this afternoon' . . . [He did so and the minister prayed over him again.] I said, 'Jesus Christ, I know you died on the cross for me. Please, I don't like who I am, please forgive me, please.' . . . As I talked I started to feel a weird feeling in my belly . . . Then I started to feel this bubbly feeling slowly coming up my body – through my legs, my chest . . . Here I was, a hard man in prison – I didn't want to cry. But it rose up and up until suddenly I began crying my eyes out.

The *Evening Gazette* concludes the story:

> My prison life changed overnight literally. My complete change of attitude meant that I was no longer being segregated, but that I was someone who could be trusted to work in the chapel as a cleaner. I even rose up to living on an enhanced living, which means your behaviour is good so you get privileges. This behaviour pattern was a surprise to both inmates and officers alike. The realisation that both I and the prison officers were equal human beings caused my attitude towards them to completely change. I no longer thought of them as the system itself, but realised they were just representatives and ordinary men doing their jobs. People who knew me during my 'previous lifestyle' knew that I had many issues with regards to prison officers and authority in general, and I would not have taken the time to speak to them or share any of my views. Both officers and inmates could see I had changed dramatically. At times I was mocked, laughed at and doubted, but I didn't care, I believe I was being tested because of my new-found faith.

There are many patterns in this dramatic story that will be familiar to anyone acquainted with conversion narratives. St Paul set the pattern and St Augustine's *Confessions* reinforced it. Such accounts typically contain black-and-white changes. A despicable life is transformed in a flash into a life that is redeemed. The reality for most of us, I suspect, is far less clear-cut and theatrical. For us faith does not suddenly emerge from nowhere and sinfulness is horribly persistent even in a life of faith.

Yet there does seem to be something important in this story. Shane Taylor evidently felt that he had been reached when he was at his most desperate and vulnerable. A person of faith had inspired him to look for and then recognize faith.

MEDITATION

Psalm 145.13

The LORD is faithful in all his words,
and gracious in all his deeds.

Sura 16.15

If you count God's blessing, you will never number it.

28

What is faith?

Then he came again to Cana in Galilee where he had changed
the water into wine. Now there was a royal official whose
son lay ill in Capernaum. When he heard that Jesus had come
from Judea to Galilee, he went and begged him to come down
and heal his son, for he was at the point of death. Then Jesus
said to him, 'Unless you see signs and wonders you will not
believe.' The official said to him, 'Sir, come down before my
little boy dies.' Jesus said to him, 'Go; your son will live.' The
man believed the word that Jesus spoke to him and started
on his way. As he was going down, his slaves met him and
told him that his child was alive. So he asked them the hour
when he began to recover, and they said to him, 'Yesterday at
one in the afternoon the fever left him.' The father realized
that this was the hour when Jesus had said to him, 'Your son
will live.' So he himself believed, along with his whole household. (John 4.46–53)

The short Greek word for 'faith' in the Gospels has a surprisingly wide set of meanings. As a verb in this story from John it
is translated as 'believe'. On occasions in the Gospels it seems to
mean simply 'agreeing' with something. It can denote 'trust', as
in trusting someone. Just occasionally, as in John's story, it seems
to refer to someone who is 'a believer', a follower of Christ, 'a
Christian'. Even within healing stories its exact meaning can be
elusive.

This healing story is for once told by John in a style very
similar to the writers of the first three Gospels. Yet it contains
a very subtle and multi-layered understanding of 'faith'. If the
story about Shane Taylor suggests a rather raw and early

moment of faith, the Fourth Gospel points to layers beyond this.

The story appears to use 'believe' in the sense of 'trust' in the sentence: 'The man believed the word that Jesus spoke to him.' In a number of the healing stories something like this could be the meaning of 'faith'. The people to be healed trusted that Jesus was indeed able to heal them. Or, simply, they had confidence (from the Latin meaning literally 'with faith') in him, and they trusted him to help them.

This basic level of trust is still crucial in health care today. If people do not trust their doctors, then doctor–patient relationships are damaged and health care is all the poorer. That might be why many doctors are so opposed to euthanasia being made legal, despite strong public pressure for change. They may fear that they will be the ones required to administer euthanasia and that vulnerable patients would then not trust them as doctors.

Some have argued, as noted earlier, that today we increasingly lack trust in anyone in positions of responsibility, let alone 'a royal official'. A culture of audit was introduced by politicians in order to bolster public trust but in reality it may have fostered public suspicion. The right of patients formally to complain about their doctors, or the right of parents to complain about teachers, has now become a burden upon professionals and might even have increased public suspicion of them. A culture of suspicion means that we are now routinely cynical about all politicians. We are surrounded by security cameras and burglar alarms, yet we feel less and less secure.

At another layer the story also contains a more mutual understanding of 'faith'. There is a pattern of request–response–request–response with another mention of 'believe'. The royal official went and begged Jesus to come down and heal his son. Jesus responded, 'Unless you see signs and wonders you will not believe.' The official continued his request, 'Sir, come down before my little boy dies.' Jesus responded again, 'Go; your son will live.'

In more paternalist times professionals were treated with some deference. It was for the doctor to decide about the patient's treatment or for the lawyer to deliver some unquestioned judgment. Students would have not thought of addressing university professors by their first names. Today we expect more mutuality than this. Doctors, we believe, should discuss treatment options with their patients, and lawyers options with their clients. I am also happy that students feel free to call me 'Robin'.

A third layer, faith as a response to God, comes at the end of the story: 'So he himself believed, along with his whole household.' For John this apparently means 'he became a Christian', as it does in the Prologue (1.7, 'so that all might believe through him') and in two out of three of the other Johannine healing stories. So, at the end of the story of the Healing of the Blind Man, the one healed exclaims 'Lord, I believe' (9.38) and proceeds to worship Jesus, and the story of the Raising of Lazarus concludes with the verse: 'Many of the Jews therefore, who had come with Mary and had seen what Jesus did, believed in him' (11.45). For all but one of these stories faith in this sense is shared with others: the royal official 'believed, along with his whole household'.

Most striking of all is the exchange between Jesus and Martha just before the raising of Lazarus:

> Jesus said to her, 'I am the resurrection and the life. Those who believe in me, even though they die, will live, and everyone who lives and believes in me will never die. Do you believe this?' She said to him, "Yes, Lord, I believe that you are the Messiah, the Son of God, the one coming into the world. (John 11.25–27)

There is nothing so elaborate as this declaration of faith within the healing stories of the other Gospels. At most there is the conclusion to the healing of the paralysed man in Mark 2.12 (including Matthew's added comment that 'they glorified God, who had given such authority to men'): 'And he stood up, and immediately took the mat and went out before all of them; so that they were all amazed and glorified God, saying, "We have never seen anything like this!"'

Faith in this fullest sense might be more important for health than is usually noticed. There is now a wealth of research suggesting that religious faith and practice are strongly associated with improved health and longevity. Some of the health benefits here may result from the healthier life-styles of the religiously active. Yet it is difficult to explain all these benefits in this way. Again it is possible that commitment to a cause of any kind may be good for health, perhaps even a strong commitment to atheism (although I am not aware that this has actually been tested).

Few religious people would regard such benefits as a good reason for being religious, and nor do any of my non-religious friends. Faced with the prospect of going to church every week in the hope of some health benefits, the latter usually joke that it is just not worth it!

The point is simpler. There does seem to be a connection between 'faith', health and wholeness at several levels.

MEDITATION

Psalm 85.10

Steadfast love and faithfulness will meet;
righteousness and peace will kiss each other.

Sura 27.60

He who guides you in the shadows of the land and the sea and looses the winds, bearing good tidings before his mercy.

29

The faith of a Gentile

When he entered Capernaum, a centurion came to him, appealing to him and saying, 'Lord, my servant is lying at home paralysed, in terrible distress.' And he said to him, 'I will come and cure him.' The centurion answered, 'Lord, I am not worthy to have you come under my roof; but only speak the word, and my servant will be healed. For I also am a man under authority, with soldiers under me; and I say to one, "Go", and he goes, and to another, "Come", and he comes, and to my slave, "Do this", and the slave does it.' When Jesus heard him, he was amazed and said to those who followed him, 'Truly I tell you, in no one in Israel have I found such faith. I tell you, many will come from east and west and will eat with Abraham and Isaac and Jacob in the kingdom of heaven, while the heirs of the kingdom will be thrown into the outer darkness, where there will be weeping and gnashing of teeth.' And to the centurion Jesus said, 'Go; let it be done for you according to your faith.' And the servant was healed in that hour. (Matthew 8.5–13)

The same story is found in Luke. Both Matthew and Luke also have similarities with John's story about the royal official. The focus in Matthew and Luke is upon the fact that this is a Gentile who comes to Jesus and receives the astonishing praise, 'Truly I tell you, in no one in Israel have I found such faith.' To emphasize this further Matthew adds, 'Go; let it be done for you according to your faith', while Luke adds that Jewish elders insisted to Jesus that this Gentile 'is worthy of having you do this for him, for he loves our people, and it is he who built our synagogue for us' (7.4–5).

Taken together, there is some ambiguity across the three Gospels both about the job of this important person and about whom it is that is to be healed. In John it is the royal official's son, in Luke it is the centurion's slave, but in Matthew it is the centurion's 'boy' (a word that could be used for either a son or a servant). Bridging the gap somewhat, Luke adds that this slave was 'valued highly' by the centurion.

Ambiguities apart, this is a very important story about faith. Jesus was amazed at the faith he found.

In Matthew there is a particularly interesting twist. On two separate occasions he portrays the mission of Jesus as being only to the Jewish people and not to Gentiles. Matthew alone has the following instruction to the twelve disciples: 'These twelve Jesus sent out with the following instructions: "Go nowhere among the Gentiles, and enter no town of the Samaritans, but go rather to the lost sheep of the house of Israel"' (10.5–6). And he adds this same point to Mark's earlier version of the remarkable story about the Syro-Phoenician/ Canaanite woman:

> A Canaanite woman from that region came out and started shouting, 'Have mercy on me, Lord, Son of David; my daughter is tormented by a demon.' But he did not answer her at all. And his disciples came and urged him, saying, 'Send her away, for she keeps shouting after us.' He answered, 'I was sent only to the lost sheep of the house of Israel.' But she came and knelt before him, saying, 'Lord, help me.' He answered, 'It is not fair to take the children's food and throw it to the dogs.' She said, 'Yes, Lord, yet even the dogs eat the crumbs that fall from their masters' table.' Then Jesus answered her, 'Woman, great is your faith! Let it be done for you as you wish.' And her daughter was healed instantly. (Matthew 15.22–28)

So it seems that, despite Matthew's general conviction that the so-called earthly ministry of Jesus was for the Jewish people alone, he tells two healing stories involving Gentiles who were especially praised by Jesus for their faith.

The Canaanite is praised effusively for her faith: 'Woman, great is your faith!' She has persisted despite the strong discouragement from the disciples and, for once, despite Jesus' own discouragement. Some have argued that this is one of the very few occasions when Jesus apparently changed his position. What is more, he changed it in response to someone who was both a woman and a Gentile (even 'a dog', a derogatory term sometimes applied to Gentiles). Others see a more playful irony in the exchange between Jesus and the woman: 'It is not fair to take the children's food and throw it to the dogs' . . . 'Yes, Lord, yet even the dogs eat the crumbs that fall from their masters' table.' However interpreted, it is finally this Gentile's faith that is important.

If Jesus in this story so recognized the faith of other religious people, perhaps we should do the same today. Perhaps Christians should be praising and learning from the faith of Jews, Muslims and others in the twenty-first century. The next chapter will return to this suggestion about what might be involved in being a bit like Jesus.

MEDITATION

Psalm 57.9–10

I will give thanks to you, O Lord, among the peoples;
I will sing praises to you among the nations.
For your steadfast love is as high as the heavens;
your faithfulness extends to the clouds.

Sura 2.170

They who fulfil their covenant when they are engaged in a covenant, and endure with fortitude misfortune, hardship and peril, these are they who are true in their faith, these are the truly godfearing.

30

Faithfulness

A doctor friend was asked to produce a set of bullet points for a patient fact sheet about healthy living. He included the obvious candidates: Don't smoke; Drink and eat moderately; Take exercise; and so forth. Then he playfully added two final bullet points: Have a happy and faithful marriage; Go to church.

Colleagues were outraged. 'You can't possibly add the last two!' He teased them further: 'The scientific evidence is pretty convincing. Happy and faithful marriages and active religious involvement can both contribute significantly to good health.'

Of course he removed them. Patients today would not take kindly to moralizing from doctors. Leave that to the clergy. My friend had made his point, although I suspect that his colleagues failed to notice the irony that it is still acceptable for doctors to moralize about smoking, etc.

Moralizing apart, faithfulness is both valued and scorned in wider society today. Whenever people are asked about the qualities that make for a happy marriage they typically mention faithfulness. Sometimes this may be interpreted too narrowly in terms simply of sexual faithfulness. Yet, in better moments, many still realize that faithfulness involves much more than that. It is demanding but it is also fulfilling.

Yet we are surrounded by unfaithfulness. Relationships, whether married or not, appear to be getting more temporary. Marriages fail or never materialize and increasingly children are not brought up by both of their biological parents. There is no need to glorify the past. Doubtless there were many unhappy marriages when divorce was more difficult. And some biological parents make dreadful fathers and mothers. Nevertheless unfaithfulness between couples and unfaithfulness of parents towards their children seem to have contributed little to our overall wellbeing today.

The themes of faith and faithfulness run strongly through the Bible. Over and again in the Old Testament it is insisted that God has been faithful to us so we should be faithful to each other and to God. Faithlessness is seen as a constant failing of weak human beings.

In the stories about Jesus faithlessness is seen in exactly the same way. The following is typical:

> When they came to the crowd, a man came to him, knelt before him, and said, 'Lord, have mercy on my son, for he is an epileptic and he suffers terribly; he often falls into the fire and often into the water. And I brought him to your disciples, but they could not cure him.' Jesus answered, 'You faithless and perverse generation, how much longer must I be with you? How much longer must I put up with you? Bring him here to me.' And Jesus rebuked the demon, and it came out of him, and the boy was cured instantly. Then the disciples came to Jesus privately and said, 'Why could we not cast it out?' He said to them, 'Because of your little faith. For truly I tell you, if you have faith the size of a mustard seed, you will say to this mountain, "Move from here to there", and it will move; and nothing will be impossible for you.' (Matthew 17.14–20)

The irony in this story about a grain of faith moving mountains has sometimes been misunderstood by naive religious groups. Faith properly understood is not about believing in things that are simply impossible. The point here is surely that faithlessness achieves little or nothing. As seen earlier, faced with faithlessness or a lack of trust even Jesus could not always heal. On the way to the cross, he was surrounded by faithlessness. He noticed and praised some remarkable faith, but he was only too aware of its absence as well.

Faith and faithfulness are fundamental to being a bit like Jesus.

———➤●◄———

MEDITATION

Psalm 119.158

I look at the faithless with disgust,
because they do not keep your commands.

Sura 39.60

God is the creator of every thing; He is the guardian over every
thing; to him belong the keys of the heavens and the earth.
And those who disbelieve in the signs of God – they are the losers.

WEEK 6

Humility

——➤●◄——

31

Commands to silence

As Jesus went on from there, two blind men followed him, crying loudly, 'Have mercy on us, Son of David!' When he entered the house, the blind men came to him; and Jesus said to them, 'Do you believe that I am able to do this?' They said to him, 'Yes, Lord.' Then he touched their eyes and said, 'According to your faith let it be done to you.' And their eyes were opened. Then Jesus sternly ordered them, 'See that no one knows of this.' But they went away and spread the news about him throughout that district.

After they had gone away, a demoniac who was mute was brought to him. And when the demon had been cast out, the one who had been mute spoke; and the crowds were amazed and said, 'Never has anything like this been seen in Israel.' But the Pharisees said, 'By the ruler of the demons he casts out the demons.'

Then Jesus went about all the cities and villages, teaching in their synagogues, and proclaiming the good news of the kingdom, and curing every disease and every sickness. When he saw the crowds, he had compassion for them, because they

were harassed and helpless, like sheep without a shepherd.
(Matthew 9.27–36)

Values already explored will readily be seen in this set of brief
healing stories. The compassion (in the visceral sense) of Jesus
is present in the final sentence and a loud cry for mercy/compassion in the first. There is care in the by-now-familiar form of
Jesus touching the blind men's eyes and then going 'about all
the cities and villages . . . curing every disease and every sickness'. And there is mention of the faith of the two blind men.

There is also something else that has been present but not as yet
noticed in previous stories. Addressing the blind men, 'Jesus
sternly ordered them, "See that no one knows of this."' The sternness has been highlighted earlier but not the command to silence.

In Mark's Gospel four healing stories conclude with a similar
command, demons are also silenced twice, and the disciples are
told to keep silent on a couple of other occasions. There has
been much speculation among scholars about the purpose of
these commands. One famous theory is that Mark himself
devised this silence in order to show that while he was on earth
Jesus kept secret the fact that he was the Messiah and revealed
this only after his resurrection.

This might just fit Mark, although it does not remotely fit the
other Gospels. Even Mark is not exactly consistent about this
supposed secrecy and, judging from the High Priest's question,
does presume that the 'secret' was well out by the time of the
trial and crucifixion.

Another theory relates to purity. For instance, Mark's story of
the 'leper' (examined in section 21) has the sentence, 'After
sternly warning him [Jesus] sent him away at once, saying to
him, "See that you say nothing to anyone; but go, show yourself
to the priest, and offer for your cleansing what Moses commanded, as a testimony to them."' It was after all the role of
the priest alone to declare someone 'clean', so it might have
appeared improper for the man to have declared anything in
public until he had been to the priest (unless, of course, Jesus
himself is seen as the priest here).

Unfortunately this explanation does not work too well with all other healing stories. In most of them there is no command or even requirement to see the priest. What is more, the story of the 'leper' contains another element that does fit the story of the two blind men. It finishes with the sentence, 'But he went out and began to proclaim it freely, and to spread the word, so that Jesus could no longer go into a town openly, but stayed out in the country; and people came to him from every quarter.' Perhaps this provides a better clue.

If a command to silence is seen as a feature of a healing story, a pattern begins to emerge. Jesus strictly commands the one who has just been healed not to tell anyone. That person then rushes out and, defying Jesus' explicit command, tells everyone. Then everyone presses to see Jesus for themselves. Jesus shows concern and distress at the crowds, 'harassed and helpless, like sheep without a shepherd', and finally is forced to withdraw. The full pattern is not present on every occasion but it is evident across several:

 healing
   restraint
      restraint broken
        frenzied crowds
         distress
           forced withdrawal

MEDITATION

Psalm 37.7

Be still before the LORD, and wait patiently for him.

Sura 7.50

Call on your LORD, humbly and secretly.

32

Jairus' daughter

When Jesus had crossed again in the boat to the other side, a great crowd gathered round him; and he was by the lake. Then one of the leaders of the synagogue named Jairus came and, when he saw him, fell at his feet and begged him repeatedly, 'My little daughter is at the point of death. Come and lay your hands on her, so that she may be made well, and live.' So he went with him. And a large crowd followed him and pressed in on him . . .

While he was still speaking, some people came from the leader's house to say, 'Your daughter is dead. Why trouble the teacher any further?' But overhearing what they said, Jesus said to the leader of the synagogue, 'Do not fear, only believe.' He allowed no one to follow him except Peter, James, and John, the brother of James. When they came to the house of the leader of the synagogue, he saw a commotion, people weeping and wailing loudly. When he had entered, he said to them, 'Why do you make a commotion and weep? The child is not dead but sleeping.' And they laughed at him. Then he put them all outside, and took the child's father and mother and those who were with him, and went in where the child was. He took her by the hand and said to her, 'Talitha cum', which means, 'Little girl, get up!' And immediately the girl got up and began to walk about (she was twelve years of age). At this they were overcome with amazement. He strictly ordered them that no one should know this, and told them to give her something to eat. (Mark 5.21–24, 35–43)

Frenzied crowds are well in evidence in this healing story from Mark. There is also the 'commotion, people weeping and wailing loudly', perhaps a band of professional mourners. The story is wrapped around the story explored in an earlier section, that of the woman 'suffering from haemorrhages for twelve years'.

It concludes with a strict order 'that no one should know this', but it also includes Jesus putting all outside except the immediate family circle. A double restraint. The healing is for these few people alone to witness, not for the edification or curiosity of the crowds. Even the few who were witnesses were commanded to silence.

Seen in this way silence was part of the restraint/reticence normally necessary within a healing context. It was not inviolable. Even in Mark the healed 'demoniac' was told by Jesus, 'Go home to your friends, and tell them how much the Lord has done for you, and what mercy he has shown you' (5.19). But, in a context of a frenzied, over-demanding and, in this instance, jeering crowd, it was both safer and more apposite.

In a context of health care today restraint, even humility, is important yet too often absent. Patients and their families can demand too much and medical science can sometimes claim too much. The combination of the two can extend health services well beyond their means and capabilities. Some patients soon learn that if they keep demanding and demanding then somebody in authority is likely eventually to give in to them, possibly at the expense of those patients who are much more needy but less demanding. With resources pushed to these limits the humble patients will then tend to be ignored, while the demanding ones might be over-treated. Damaging for both groups of patients.

Medical science can also claim too much. For the last eight years I have been a member of stem cell monitoring committees. Some religious people object very strongly to embryonic research in this area. I understand their views but do not share them. I believe that there are important compassionate reasons for supporting stem cell research in the hope that one day this will benefit patients with very serious degenerative diseases or inherited conditions.

Nevertheless, stem cell research is still in its infancy and some of the therapeutic claims made for it are well beyond present possibilities. Public pressure and a need to secure grants for such research can sometimes encourage medical scientists to exaggerate just how imminent and widespread therapy really is.

Humility in health care is important at many different levels.

———————

MEDITATION

Psalm 119.67

Before I was humbled I went astray . . .

Sura 16.125

And be patient: yet is your patience only with the help of God.

33

Morris Cerullo's healing mission to London

In the early 1990s a great deal of publicity was given to the work of the American evangelist Morris Cerullo. Many in England at the time were unfamiliar with the so-called Prosperity Gospel, according to which if you are righteous then God will give you wealth, health and eternal salvation. At that stage it was more commonly encountered in the southern states in America than in Britain. Today it can readily be found in parts of London as well.

One of the striking features of the Prosperity Gospel is that pastors often have a more luxurious life-style than impoverished members of their congregations. They promise these members healing and salvation and ask them in return to tithe their modest incomes. If challenged they often claim that wealth (their own included) is a sign of God's blessing.

Morris Cerullo first set up an independent ministry in 1961, working from a garage in San Diego. In 1990 he acquired Global Satellite Network (formerly owned by the now disgraced evangelist Jim Bakker). By 1992 his publishing and broadcasting network was valued at £27,000,000 and he was holding evangelistic crusades in more than 70 countries, with a humble ambition to 'win a billion souls' by 2000.

During the summer of 1992 his Mission to London launched an advertising campaign with billboards placed at various strategic points around London and publicity given out in many local evangelical and Pentecostal churches. Posters featured discarded white canes and overturned wheelchairs and carried the caption:

Some Will see Miracles for the First Time

By October, after investigating complaints, the Advertising Standards Authority found that the posters had been 'targeted on the disabled' and were 'a source of distress'.

In her study of Morris Cerullo, Nancy Schaefer describes in detail a typical day at his Mission to London in August 1994. It lasted from 10 a.m. to 10 p.m. and apparently attracted a predominantly Afro-Caribbean following. The start of the day consisted of a variety of booths in the exhibition hall selling Christian books, videos, T-shirts and bumper-stickers, among other similar items. At 11.30 a.m. there was a service of singing and intercessory prayers, 'followed by personal testimonials of miraculous healing given by a different individual each day'. Then followed four consecutive hour-long teaching sessions 'which covered topics ranging from eschatology and adventism to generational curses and spiritual warfare'. The healing service itself, open to a wider public, was held in the evening. At this Morris Cerullo played the central role, talking 'in a folksy vernacular . . . main points are repeated in easy-to-remember phrases ("The Devil is a liar") and are illustrated in stories rather than defended through complex theological argument':

> As the service progresses, the milieu begins to change perceptively. At first the American speaks slowly in a quiet voice but gradually increases the tempo and volume of his delivery, until he virtually shouts at the top of his voice in rapid successive bursts. The crowd roars its approval on cues given by him and they respond enthusiastically with shouts of 'Amen' and 'Thank you Jesus'. At times the cacophony in the hall is almost deafening as some exuberant attendees become 'slain in the Spirit'. They shout, laugh, weep, dance, wave, clap, collapse, speak in tongues and cast out demonic spirits . . . Meanwhile Cerullo describes the outpouring of the Holy Spirit as 'liquid fire' and calls out ailments which purportedly are being healed . . . He then proceeds to give out the invitation to come forward (the altar call) and asks those who have been healed to come on the stage. Individuals then give their

personal testimonials in turn; Cerullo prays and lays hands over each one. Ordinarily people collapse when touched and volunteers stand by to catch them as they fall. This portion of the service can be quite lengthy depending upon the number of people who come forward . . . Cerullo usually allows anywhere [between] twelve or more testimonials before concluding the service. A closing hymn is then sung but one which is quiet and calming rather than loud and rousing as sung at the outset. (Nancy A. Schaefer, 'Making the Rulers Tremble!: Morris Cerullo World Evangelism's 1994 Mission to London Revival', in Marion Bowman (ed.), *Healing and Religion*, Hisarlik Press, Enfield Lock, Middlesex, 2000, pp. 27–28)

The difference between this and the Gospels' command to silence is striking. For Morris Cerullo maximum publicity, sensational advertising, animated crowds and a carefully orchestrated healing service were crucial. There was no order from him to 'tell no one'. There were no crowds put out of the room while the vulnerable were healed in private. Healing was on a public stage in a large hall with excited friends and relatives singing, dancing and shouting. And, of course, there was no attempt to escape from the pressing crowds and exaggerated claims to find a place of solitude for prayer.

The crowds did not need to go hunting for Morris Cerullo, he was already seeking them. There were also considerable amounts of money involved and an extensive commercial empire.

In short, the reticence and humility of Jesus in the context of healing was replaced with vociferous and systematic boasts claiming that 'Some Will see Miracles for the First Time'.

Contrast this with the restraint Jesus shows in Luke's story (4.40–42):

As the sun was setting, all those who had any who were sick with various kinds of diseases brought them to him; and he laid his hands on each of them and cured them. Demons also came out of many, shouting, 'You are the Son of God!' But he rebuked them and would not allow them to speak, because they knew that he was the Messiah.

At daybreak he departed and went into a deserted place. And the crowds were looking for him; and when they reached him, they wanted to prevent him from leaving them.

———⟫●⟪———

MEDITATION

Psalm 25.9

[God] leads the humble in what is right,
and teaches the humble his way.

Sura 4.95

God has been gracious to you. So be discriminating; surely God is aware of the things you do.

34

Reversing the Prosperity Gospel

One of the dinner guests, on hearing this, said to him, 'Blessed is anyone who will eat bread in the kingdom of God!' Then Jesus said to him, 'Someone gave a great dinner and invited many. At the time for the dinner he sent his slave to say to those who had been invited, "Come; for everything is ready now." But they all alike began to make excuses. The first said to him, "I have bought a piece of land, and I must go out and see it; please accept my apologies." Another said, "I have bought five yoke of oxen, and I am going to try them out; please accept my apologies." Another said, "I have just been married, and therefore I cannot come." So the slave returned and reported this to his master. Then the owner of the house became angry and said to his slave, "Go out at once into the streets and lanes of the town and bring in the poor, the crippled, the blind, and the lame." And the slave said, "Sir, what you ordered has been done, and there is still room." Then the master said to the slave, "Go out into the roads and lanes, and compel people to come in, so that my house may be filled. For I tell you, none of those who were invited will taste my dinner."' (Luke 14.15–24)

Both Luke and Matthew tell this splendidly exaggerated parable about a great dinner (it is a wedding banquet in Matthew). Who could refuse such an invitation? But Matthew confuses things by adding to it a different parable about a man who does attend yet is not wearing a wedding robe and is then 'thrown out into the outer darkness' (a bit tough when presumably he had been pressganged into attending in the first place).

For Luke this seems to be a parable about the kingdom which reverses our usual values. The excuses of the invited guests to the kingdom of God are contrasted with the invitations instead to 'the poor, the crippled, the blind, and the lame'.

If Morris Cerullo represents the Prosperity Gospel, Luke typically does not. Of all the Gospel writers Luke has the strongest sayings about wealth. He seems to be both familiar with wealth and also aware of its power to corrupt. Luke alone gives us Mary's song of praise (the Magnificat) with its powerful theme of reversal:

And Mary said,

'My soul magnifies the Lord,
   and my spirit rejoices in God my Saviour,
for he has looked with favour on the lowliness of his servant.
   Surely, from now on all generations will call me blessed;
for the Mighty One has done great things for me,
   and holy is his name.
His mercy is for those who fear him
   from generation to generation.
He has shown strength with his arm;
   he has scattered the proud in the thoughts of their hearts.
He has brought down the powerful from their thrones,
   and lifted up the lowly;
he has filled the hungry with good things,
   and sent the rich away empty . . .' (Luke 1.46–53)

Matthew's first beatitude, 'Blessed are the poor in spirit', is simply 'Blessed are the poor' in Luke. It is Luke alone (4.18) who gives us Jesus' sermon in the synagogue (discussed earlier) in which Jesus uses Isaiah to proclaim:

The Spirit of the Lord is upon me,
   because he has anointed me
      to bring good news to the poor.
He has sent me to proclaim release to the captives
   and recovery of sight to the blind,
      to let the oppressed go free . . .

Ironically, Luke and Acts (probably by the same author) also demonstrate a sophisticated knowledge about wealth. Luke alone has the strange command to the disciples to take a purse and bag and sell their cloaks to buy a sword (22.36). Yet it is also only Luke who warns: 'But woe to you who are rich' (6.24). And the proud and the wealthy, along with the hypocrites, are firmly told: 'Take care! Be on your guard against all kinds of greed; for one's life does not consist in the abundance of possessions' (12.15).

In contrast, as in Mark, it is the humble widow who is commended:

He looked up and saw rich people putting their gifts into the treasury; he also saw a poor widow put in two small copper coins. He said, 'Truly I tell you, this poor widow has put in more than all of them; for all of them have contributed out of their abundance, but she out of her poverty has put in all she had to live on.' (Luke 21.1–4)

This quiet and humble act of generosity is the very opposite to religious hypocrisy. We have come full circle. This really is a bit like Jesus.

———————

MEDITATION

Psalm 41.1

Happy are those who consider the poor;
the LORD delivers them in the day of trouble.

Sura 2.170

Give of one's substance, however cherished, to kinsmen, and orphans, the needy, the traveller, beggars, and . . . ransom the slave.

35

Humility between faiths

From there he set out and went away to the region of Tyre. He
entered a house and did not want anyone to know he was
there. Yet he could not escape notice, but a woman whose
little daughter had an unclean spirit immediately heard about
him, and she came and bowed down at his feet. Now the
woman was a Gentile, of Syrophoenician origin. She begged
him to cast the demon out of her daughter. He said to her,
'Let the children be fed first, for it is not fair to take the children's food and throw it to the dogs.' But she answered him,
'Sir, even the dogs under the table eat the children's crumbs.'
Then he said to her, 'For saying that, you may go – the demon
has left your daughter.' So she went home, found the child
lying on the bed, and the demon gone.

Then he returned from the region of Tyre, and went by way
of Sidon towards the Sea of Galilee, in the region of the
Decapolis. They brought to him a deaf man who had an
impediment in his speech; and they begged him to lay his
hand on him. He took him aside in private, away from the
crowd, and put his fingers into his ears, and he spat and
touched his tongue. Then looking up to heaven, he sighed and
said to him, 'Ephphatha', that is, 'Be opened.' And immediately his ears were opened, his tongue was released, and he
spoke plainly. Then Jesus ordered them to tell no one; but the
more he ordered them, the more zealously they proclaimed
it. They were astounded beyond measure, saying, 'He has
done everything well; he even makes the deaf to hear and the
mute to speak.' (Mark 7.24–37)

Matthew's parallel story of the Canaanite woman has already been analysed in section 29 to illustrate faith. Mark's version makes no mention of faith. It appears instead to have more to do with humility, especially when set alongside the story that follows it.

The story starts with Jesus seeking anonymity: 'He entered a house and did not want anyone to know he was there.' Immediately before this he had been hassled by the Pharisees about his disciples eating 'with defiled hands'. And just before that he had been pursued by another frenzied crowd:

> When they had crossed over, they came to land at Gennesaret and moored the boat. When they got out of the boat, people at once recognized him, and rushed about that whole region and began to bring the sick on mats to wherever they heard he was. And wherever he went, into villages or cities or farms, they laid the sick in the market-places, and begged him that they might touch even the fringe of his cloak; and all who touched it were healed. (Mark 6.53–56)

Yet he still 'could not escape notice'. A woman with a sick daughter 'immediately heard about him, and she came and bowed down at his feet'. Unfortunately this woman, humbling herself in submission to Jesus, was both an outsider by country and a Gentile or 'pagan' (the word used literally means 'a Greek') by religion.

The repartee exchanged between Jesus and the woman will already be familiar, striking some readers as hurtful and others as ironic. Yet Mark seems to indicate more clearly than Matthew that Jesus really did shift his position as a result of this exchange. Here he responds: 'For saying that, you may go – the demon has left your daughter.' A combination of her humble trust and self-deprecating humour appears to have convinced him to act when he otherwise might not have done so.

Restraint (and then restraint defied) continues in the story that follows. The pattern is by now thoroughly familiar: 'Jesus ordered them to tell no one; but the more he ordered them, the more zealously they proclaimed it.' And Jesus was once again faced with a 'great crowd', but this time a crowd 'without anything to eat'.

There is also an obvious difference between the two stories. The second involved fellow Jews whereas the first involved a Gentile. However, Jews and Gentile alike were healed. But it was the Gentile who caused Jesus to change.

If Jesus could change in relationship to a humble religious outsider, why cannot Christians around the world act similarly today? At a time of heightened religious conflict it has become vital that religious people behave more humbly and even learn from each other.

If Jesus as seen in section 29 could respect the faith of a humble Roman centurion, then why cannot Christians respect genuine faith in other religious traditions as well? Of course many Christians can, but sadly others cannot.

Perhaps respect for other faiths when genuine will one day be recognized as being a bit like Jesus.

MEDITATION

Psalm 149.4

For the LORD takes pleasure in his people;
he adorns the humble with victory.

Sura 23.1

Prosperous are the believers who in their prayers are humble.

36

Humility and justice

He also told this parable to some who trusted in themselves that they were righteous and regarded others with contempt: 'Two men went up to the temple to pray, one a Pharisee and the other a tax-collector. The Pharisee, standing by himself, was praying thus, "God, I thank you that I am not like other people: thieves, rogues, adulterers, or even like this tax-collector. I fast twice a week; I give a tenth of all my income." But the tax-collector, standing far off, would not even look up to heaven, but was beating his breast and saying, "God, be merciful to me, a sinner!" I tell you, this man went down to his home justified rather than the other; for all who exalt themselves will be humbled, but all who humble themselves will be exalted.' (Luke 18.9–14)

One final and extremely important connection – between humility and justice.

This is a rather unusual 'parable': it is more like a cartoon. The two men are contrasted in a stylized and exaggerated manner. Pharisees are not usually portrayed in a good light in the Gospels. In reality they were a lay movement seeking to express holiness through strict and, some would consider, fastidious observance of Jewish Law. Tax-collectors, on the other hand, were native agents for the oppressive Roman Empire. As a result, in rabbinic writings, tax-collectors were sometimes referred to as 'thieves'. Understandably both groups could be unpopular with the general public at the time.

In this sketch they represent quite opposite ways of trying to serve God. The Pharisee is the one who regards himself as righteous but actually 'regarded others with contempt'. And it is the humble and repentant tax-collector who finally 'went down to his home justified'.

Matthew puts flesh on this connection between humility and justice in his long-cherished version of the Beatitudes:

When Jesus saw the crowds, he went up the mountain; and after he sat down, his disciples came to him. Then he began to speak, and taught them, saying:

'Blessed are the poor in spirit, for theirs is the kingdom of heaven.

'Blessed are those who mourn, for they will be comforted.

'Blessed are the meek, for they will inherit the earth.

'Blessed are those who hunger and thirst for righteousness, for they will be filled.

'Blessed are the merciful, for they will receive mercy.

'Blessed are the pure in heart, for they will see God.

'Blessed are the peacemakers, for they will be called children of God . . .' (Matthew 5.1–9)

Many have turned to these Beatitudes in order to discern what it is to be a bit like Jesus. Beatitudes feature in both the ancient world and in the Old Testament, and Isaiah 61 appears to be a strong influence upon Matthew's Beatitudes (although 'peacemakers' are absent from this chapter of Isaiah). In one form or another Beatitudes have long been used to encourage faith and faithfulness.

Like many of the parables the exact meaning of some of Matthew's Beatitudes remains elusive. What does 'poor in spirit' really mean? Or 'pure in heart'? There have been many different explanations.

One approach is to see them as poetry. Taken together they make connections even if these connections cannot be translated into exact prose. Good poetry reduced to prose is usually impoverished. Or perhaps they are like a great painting, offering a vision of what it is like to be a bit like Jesus. Seen in this way they continue to speak to people across centuries and generations. The two missing verses have also been crucial to people of faith in times of persecution across different cultures.

One of the connections that might be glimpsed in the Beatitudes is between humility on the one hand and compassion and justice on the other. The poor in spirit, pure in heart, meek and those who mourn are also the ones who hunger and thirst for righteousness, are merciful and peacemakers.

A fuller and more demanding picture begins to emerge about what it is to be a bit like Jesus.

This picture starts with compassion:

- identifying someone as being in real need
- feeling strongly for that person
- being determined to help that person in any way possible.

It continues with care – passionate care for and about another person in real need.

In health care today this, in turn, involves proper respect for the other person. When capable people are offered treatment, they should surely be enabled to make informed choices, to know about the risks and benefits involved and to have confidences kept.

Faith is important: trust in each other, faithful living and, for the religious at least, faithfulness to God. These different layers of faith are intimately linked.

Justice, itself a form of compassion at a social level, is also vital – being fair to others in an often unfair world.

Finally, humility . . .
  recognizing our own obvious limitations . . .
    frail human beings . . .
      struggling to be . . .
        a bit like Jesus.

MEDITATION

Psalm 8.3–5

When I look at your heavens, the work of your fingers,
the moon and the stars that you have established;
what are human beings that you are mindful of them,
mortals that you care for them?
Yet you have made them a little lower than God,
and crowned them with glory and honour.

Sura 24.35

God is the light of the heavens and the earth.